W9-BPM-080

Cause & Effect: ANCIENT CIVILIZATIONS

Cause & Effect: Ancient Egypt

Don Nardo

ReferencePoint Press®

San Diego, CA

© 2018 ReferencePoint Press, Inc.
Printed in the United States

For more information, contact:
ReferencePoint Press, Inc.
PO Box 27779
San Diego, CA 92198
www.ReferencePointPress.com

ALL RIGHTS RESERVED.
No part of this work covered by the copyright hereon may be reproduced or used in any form or by any means—graphic, electronic, or mechanical, including photocopying, recording, taping, web distribution, or information storage retrieval systems—without the written permission of the publisher.

LIBRARY OF CONGRESS CATALOGING-IN-PUBLICATION DATA

Name: Nardo, Don, 1947- author.
Title: Cause & Effect: Ancient Egypt/By Don Nardo.
Description: San Diego, CA: ReferencePoint Press, Inc., 2018. | Series:
  Cause & effect: ancient civilizations | Includes bibliographical
  references | Audience: Grade 9-12.
Identifiers: LCCN 2016045977 (print) | LCCN 2016048043 (ebook) | ISBN
  9781682821503 (hardback) | ISBN 9781682821510 (eBook)
Subjects: LCSH: Egypt--Civilization--Juvenile literature. |
  Egypt--History--To 332 B.C.--Juvenile literature. | Egypt--History--332-30
  B.C.--Juvenile literature.
Classification: LCC DT83 .N36 2018 (print) | LCC DT83 (ebook) | DDC
  932/.01--dc23
LC record available at https://lccn.loc.gov/2016045977

CONTENTS

"History is a complex study of the many causes that have influenced happenings of the past and the complicated effects of those varied causes."

—William & Mary School of Education,
Center for Gifted Education

Understanding the causes and effects of historical events and time periods is rarely simple. The largest and most influential empire of ancient India, for instance, came into existence largely because of a series of events set in motion by Persian and Greek invaders. Although the Mauryan Empire was both wealthy and well organized and benefited enormously from strong rulers and administrators, the disarray sowed by invading forces created an opening for one of India's most ambitious and successful ancient rulers—Chandragupta, the man who later came to be known in the West as the "Indian Julius Caesar." Had conditions in India at the time been different, the outcome might have been something else altogether.

The value of analyzing cause and effect in the context of ancient civilizations, therefore, is not necessarily to identify a single cause for a singular event. The real value lies in gaining a greater understanding of that civilization as a whole and being able to recognize the many factors that gave shape and direction to its rise, its development, its fall, and its lasting importance. As outlined by the National Center for History in the Schools at the University of California–Los Angeles, these factors include "the importance of the individual in history . . . the influence of ideas, human interests, and beliefs; and . . . the role of chance, the accidental and the irrational."

ReferencePoint's Cause & Effect: Ancient Civilizations series examines some of the world's most interesting and important civilizations by focusing on various causes and consequences. For instance, in *Cause & Effect: Ancient India*, a chapter explores how one Indian ruler helped transform Buddhism into a world religion. And in *Cause & Effect: Ancient Egypt*, one chapter delves into the importance of the Nile River in the development of Egyptian civilization. Every book in the series includes thoughtful discussion of questions like these—supported by facts, examples, and a mix of fully documented primary and secondary source quotes. Each title also includes an overview of the civilization so that readers have a broad context for understanding the more detailed discussions of causes and their effects.

The value of such study is not limited to the classroom; it can also be applied to many areas of contemporary life. The ability to analyze and interpret history's causes and consequences is a form of critical thinking. Critical thinking is crucial in many professions, ranging from law enforcement to science. Critical thinking is also essential for developing an educated citizenry that fully understands the rights and obligations of living in a free society. The ability to sift through and analyze complex processes and events and identify their possible outcomes enables people in that society to make important decisions.

The Cause & Effect: Ancient Civilizations series has two primary goals. One is to help students think more critically about the human societies that once populated our world and develop a true understanding of their complexities. The other is to help build a foundation for those students to become fully participating members of the society in which they live.

IMPORTANT EVENTS IN THE HISTORY OF ANCIENT EGYPT

ca. BCE 10,000–9000
Agriculture begins in the Fertile Crescent, an arc-shaped region lying along the northern rim of the Mesopotamian plains.

ca. 6000
Migrants from other parts of the Middle East enter Egypt, bringing with them knowledge of large-scale agriculture.

ca. 3100
Two Egyptian kingdoms, the Red Land and White Land, are united into the world's first nation-state by the first pharaoh, Narmer.

ca. 2589
Khufu, builder of the Great Pyramid at Giza, ascends Egypt's throne.

ca. 1352–1336
The pharaoh Amenhotep IV changes his name to Akhenaten and launches a religious revolution based on monotheism.

ca. 1550
Egypt's New Kingdom, in which a series of vigorous pharaohs create an Egyptian empire, begins.

BCE **8000** / **3000** **2500** **2000** **1500**

ca. 4000
Egyptian farmers begin to exploit the yearly floods of the Nile River to irrigate their crops.

ca. 2055
Egypt's Middle Kingdom period begins.

ca. 1458
Thutmose III, one of Egypt's most ambitious and successful warrior-pharaohs, becomes Egypt's sole ruler.

ca. 2686
The period known as the Old Kingdom, during which Egypt's largest pyramids are built, begins.

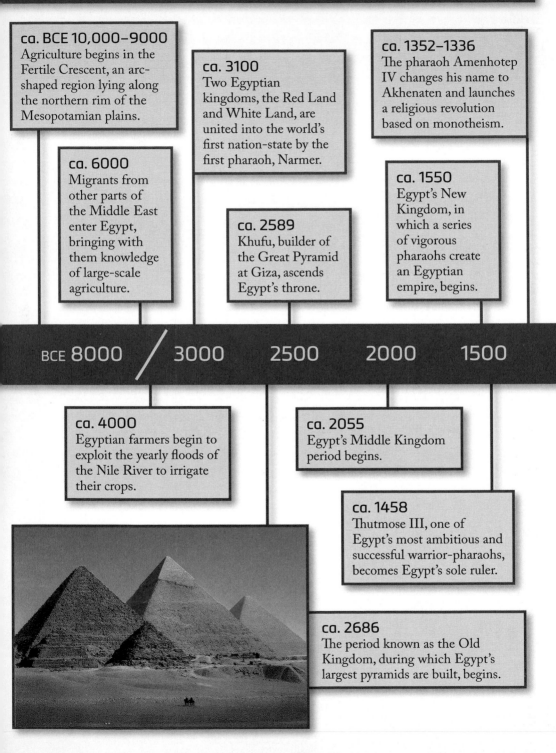

ca. 1274
The pharaoh Ramesses II fights the Hittites in a huge battle near Kadesh, in southern Syria.

31
Cleopatra VII, last of the Ptolemies and Egypt's last independent pharaoh, is defeated by Octavian (later Augustus, the first Roman emperor) at Actium, in Greece.

525
The Persians defeat the Egyptians at Pelusium, in the eastern Nile Delta, and take over Egypt.

ca. 753
The founding of Rome, on the Tiber River in western Italy, is traditionally described as occurring on this date.

1000	800	600	400	200

ca. 747–332
Members of foreign-born dynasties rule Egypt during most of this period, known as the Late Period.

323–30
Alexander's administrator, Ptolemy, and his descendants rule Egypt during these years, known as the Ptolemaic Period.

ca. 100
Julius Caesar is born; he will become an accomplished Roman leader and the lover and ally of Egypt's last pharaoh, Queen Cleopatra.

The Battle of the Animals

The date was 525 BCE, a little more than 2,540 years ago. The place was an open plain near the Egyptian village of Pelusium, in the far eastern sector of the Nile River's vast, moist, and fertile delta. The reigning pharaoh (the ancient Egyptian word for *king*), Psametik III, stood ready with a large army. Not long before, word had come that the Persian monarch, Cambyses II, was marching toward the delta with a massive army of his own.

The Persians, who had emerged from obscurity in southern Iran only three decades before, had already conquered large portions of the Middle East. Now, to Psametik's dismay, they had set their sights on defeating and absorbing his beloved native land. Egypt lacked the major political influence and strong military forces it had possessed centuries before in its heyday, what modern scholars call the New Kingdom (ca. 1550–1070 BCE). Yet the Egyptian realm was still an independent state inhabited by a proud people. Indeed, Psametik's warriors, known for their bravery, were ready to fight to the death to defend their country.

> "All the residents of a house where a cat has died a natural death shave their eyebrows, and when a dog dies they shave the whole body."[1]
>
> —Fifth-century BCE Greek historian Herodotus

The Most Devout of All Peoples

In all likelihood that is exactly what those Egyptian soldiers would have done that fateful day at Pelusium, had Cambyses not decided to play dirty. His spies had penetrated Egyptian society well in advance of the invasion, and they had informed him of an unusual aspect of the Egyptians' religious beliefs. Namely, they revered certain animals so much that they would do anything to keep them from harm.

Although Cambyses had not known beforehand about this particular oddity of the Egyptian belief system, it did not surprise him. Like everyone else in the known world at the time, he knew that the Egyptians were a religiously devout people. According to the fifth-century BCE Greek historian Herodotus, in fact, they were far and away the most devout of all peoples. Moreover, during a long visit to Egypt, Herodotus learned about their extreme dedication to certain animals that they and their gods held sacred, particularly cats and dogs. In his now famous history book he stated,

> What happens when a house catches fire is most extraordinary. Nobody takes the least trouble to put it out, for it is only the cats that matter. Everyone stands in a row, a little distance from his neighbor, trying to protect the cats, who nevertheless slip through the line, or jump over it, and hurl themselves into the flames. This causes the Egyptians deep distress. All the residents of a house where a cat has died a natural death shave their eyebrows, and when a dog dies they shave the whole body, including the head.[1]

Statuettes of the cat-goddess Bastet and other cat figurines offer a reminder of the importance of cats in ancient Egypt. Cats, dogs, hawks, and many other animals were sacred to the ancient Egyptians.

Herodotus went on to explain that the Egyptians embalmed dead cats and dogs and placed them in specially made caskets, which they buried with the highest honors. Also, though not seen to be quite as holy as cats and dogs, some other animals were held to be almost as special and blessed by the Egyptian gods. These included hawks, ibises, mice, bears, and wolves. Furthermore, Herodotus explained, in some sectors of Egypt crocodiles, hippos, otters, and certain snakes and fish were also considered sacred.

A Sinister Plan

Having heard these same things from his spies, Cambyses hatched a sinister plan to use that peculiar religious concept of the Egyptians against them. First, he had his artists paint images of the Egyptian cat-goddess, Bastet, on his soldiers' shields. Next, according to the second-century CE Greek historian Polyaenus, the Persian king placed "before his front battle line dogs, cats, ibises, and whatever other animals the Egyptians hold sacred."[2]

Thus, as the battle commenced and the Egyptian fighters charged forward at the enemy, they soon saw, to their shock and horror, thousands of their holiest creatures arrayed before them. This turn of events slowed and quickly halted the Egyptian charge. Large numbers of Pharaoh Psametik's troops were suddenly in an awful quandary. Should they continue the attack and in so doing condemn all those sacred beasts to certain death? Or should they obey what they saw as the will of their gods to spare those animals at all costs?

"[The Persian king] captured Pelusium, and thereby opened up for himself the route into Egypt."[3]

—Second-century CE Greek historian Polyaenus

Most of the soldiers chose the second option—to preserve the sacred creatures. The battle would be lost, they surely realized. But that must have seemed trivial to them in the face of the divine wrath they thought would descend on and utterly destroy Egypt if they allowed those beasts to die. Therefore, as Polyaenus wrote, "The Egyptians immediately stopped their operations, out of fear of hurting the animals."

As a result, as the sly Cambyses had hoped would happen, he "captured Pelusium, and thereby opened up for himself the route into Egypt."[3]

According to Herodotus, after fleeing Pelusium, Psametik and his soldiers "shut themselves up" in their city of Memphis. "Cambyses called upon them to come to terms,"[4] but they refused to negotiate. So the Persians laid siege to Memphis, eventually forcing the inhabitants to surrender. In this way, in a classic example of historical cause and effect, a deeply held religious belief helped to reduce an independent Egypt to domination by Persian overlords. Even worse for the Egyptians, the Persians were destined to be only the first of several foreign powers that would rule Egypt for the remainder of the ancient era.

CHAPTER ONE

A Brief History of Ancient Egypt

Modern scholars identify ancient Egypt as one of the four so-called cradles of civilization. (The other three arose in Mesopotamia—now Iraq—India, and China.) Exactly when the initial sparks of that civilization, which grew up along the banks of the Nile River, first ignited remains unclear. Some evidence shows that small groups of people entered the Nile Valley sometime between fifty thousand and one hundred thousand years ago. They were hunter-gatherers who sustained themselves by hunting; fishing; and gathering roots, berries, and various wild plants. They also lived either in caves, where available, or crude huts made of river reeds and tree branches. These earliest Egyptians lacked knowledge of farming and had no towns, writing skills, sophisticated arts and crafts, or political organization. So they did not yet possess what historians recognize as a full-fledged civilization.

Agriculture as a Trigger

This situation started to change shortly after 6000 BCE (around eight thousand years ago). During this period some migrants from Mesopotamia and what are now Syria, Jordan, and Israel crossed the Sinai Peninsula into northeastern Egypt. These newcomers were not hunter-gatherers. Rather, they knew the rudiments of agriculture, which had arisen in their home regions about three thousand years before. It appears that they introduced their simple but effective farming methods to the people who dwelled along the shores of Faiyum Lake, lying a few miles southwest of the Nile Delta. Soon emmer wheat, barley, and possibly flax grew in profusion in what was, at the time, a well-watered area. The residents also began raising sheep, pigs, and other types of livestock. During the centuries immediately following this milestone in Egyptian history, knowledge of growing crops and raising domesticated animals steadily spread through the fertile lands bordering the Nile's long, twisting ribbon of life-giving water. Beyond that narrow band, more than 90 percent of Egypt's land was—as remains the case today—arid, inhospitable desert.

Historians are unsure when Egyptian farmers learned to take full advantage of the Nile's annual floods. Each year the river gently overflows its banks, not only irrigating the nearby flatlands, but also laying down a fresh layer of extremely rich soil. Certainly by 4000 BCE large-scale agriculture using this natural boon was in full swing along several hundred miles of the river to the south of its massive, fan-shaped delta.

Most modern experts employ that approximate date to mark the emergence of a true civilization in Egypt. In large part this was because the development of large-scale agriculture triggered the adoption of other aspects of civilized life. For example, having reliable long-term food sources stimulated the growth of small villages and towns across the fertile sections of the Nile Valley. In turn, close cooperation among townspeople spurred new ideas, both practical and artistic. These included making metal tools and weapons and learning to fashion all sorts of useful pottery objects, stone sculptures, and wall paintings.

The World's First Nation

These advances were accompanied by increasing political organization, at first on the village level and later on a larger scale. At some point in the early 3000s BCE, groups of neighboring villages began coming together to form small province-like units, each called a *sepat*. The Greeks later came to call them *nomes*, the name they are best known by today. Each nome was administered by a leader known as a *nomarch*.

In time, there were forty-two nomes in Egypt—twenty in the north, around the delta and nearby areas, and twenty-two lying farther south. As political experimentation continued, each of the two groups of nomes grew into a small realm ruled by a king. The northern kingdom became known as the Red Land, and its southern counterpart was the White Land.

In part because the Egyptians did not yet keep written historical records, modern scholars know almost nothing about these realms and their leaders. What is known is that the Red and White Lands developed a healthy rivalry that led to hostilities, possibly including all-out wars for supremacy. There were also calls for peace and unification, as

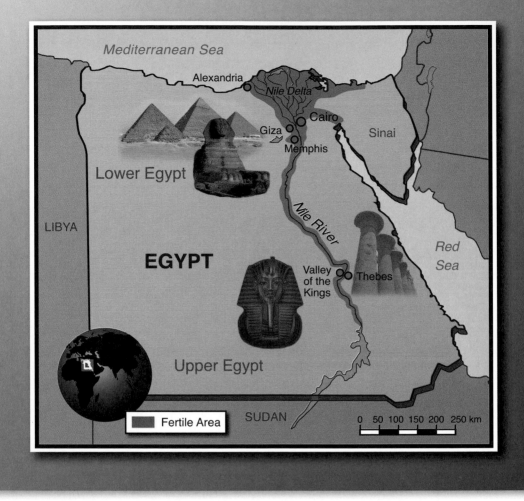

evidenced by a watershed event that occurred around 3100 BCE. A king of the White Land, Narmer, united the two sections of Egypt into a single, powerful nation-state, the first known example of a centralized country in human history.

Taking the title of *pharaoh*, Narmer built a new capital city, Memphis, a bit north of the boundary between the former rival kingdoms. He also chose a second-in-command, a kind of chief administrator—the vizier—a post destined to remain in place during most of the rest of the country's ancient period. In addition the first pharaoh introduced a crown that merged the primary features of the crowns worn by the kings of the Red and White Lands. Every later pharaoh, including the last—the famous Cleopatra—would don this same distinctive symbol of power and majesty.

Indeed, the Egyptian pharaoh was seen as the nation's supreme authority figure. His or her word was law; he or she was also the commander of the national army. Moreover, the pharaoh came to be seen as having a direct connection to the gods the Egyptians worshiped. As one modern expert puts it, the pharaoh was "regarded as the living descendant of the sun god. A pharaoh acquired this deified status upon his coronation."[5] To the average Egyptian, the nation's leader had "the aura of a divine being," remarks noted scholar H.W.F. Saggs. "Because the king was an incarnate god, with Egypt's welfare in his care, it was in everyone's interest to conform to his will."[6]

> "Because the king was an incarnate god, with Egypt's welfare in his care, it was in everyone's interest to conform to his will."[6]
>
> —Historian H.W.F. Saggs

The Old Kingdom and Pyramid Builders

The ancient Egyptian nation therefore started out with some important inherent strengths. First, it enjoyed an abundant food supply provided by the work of tens of thousands of farmers tending the well-irrigated lands lying along the Nile's banks. Second, thanks to the nomes and the two early kingdoms that grew from them, Egypt possessed an already long-standing tradition of well-organized government administration. In addition the new nation could boast of having firm, trustworthy leadership because its king was seen as divinely inspired and therefore more than worthy of devotion and obedience. These strengths at least in part explain why ancient Egyptian civilization prospered, in the face of numerous odds, for close to three millennia.

For the sake of convenience, modern experts divide that long era into several time periods. The Early Dynastic Period, for instance, lasted from the unification in 3100 to about 2686 BCE. Then came one of the country's most important and memorable periods—the Old Kingdom (ca. 2686–2181 BCE). Archaeologists have confirmed that most Old Kingdom pharaohs were strong leaders who commanded much respect from their subjects.

Part of the proof for this is the fact that historians sometimes also call this period the "Pyramid Age." It was during these years that a number of pharaohs erected gigantic pyramid-shaped tombs for themselves. Each of the largest ones—still standing at Giza, in modern Cairo's western outskirts—is made up of millions of huge stone blocks. Clearly, these and the era's other immense building projects required strong leadership and a stable government. To carry out the work, leaders had to gather together "thousands of people," scholar Dieter Arnold explains. "These people had to be trained, fed, and clothed." All this "was masterminded and then enforced by the pharaoh, with his priests and officials."[7] The fruits of these labors, the giant pyramid-tombs, became and remain today striking symbols of ancient Egypt and its many impressive achievements.

The national stability that allowed untold numbers of free Egyptians to raise these mammoth monuments began to fade toward the end of the Old Kingdom. Part of this was due to droughts and famines that sapped national resources. There was also a decline in the quality of the country's kings, viziers, and other leaders. Thanks to these and other factors, in about 2180 BCE the central government partially lost control of a number of provinces and a period of disunity ensued.

The Middle Kingdom

Fortunately for the Egyptians, this time of trouble was relatively brief. In about 2055 BCE a strong pharaoh, Mentuhotep II, came to power in the city of Thebes (on the Nile in south-central Egypt) and swiftly reunited the nation. Modern experts called the more stable and fruitful period that followed the Middle Kingdom (ca. 2055–1650 BCE).

Mentuhotep's reign was long and productive. In a way it set a pattern because a majority of his immediate successors on the throne were vigorous, well-meaning rulers. They initiated a number of large-scale building projects, most notably what would eventually become the biggest temple complex in the country—at Karnak, near Thebes. They also expanded the number of farms in Egypt, increased the volume of trade with foreign nations, and encouraged learning. (The latter was true mainly in upper-class circles. The bulk of the population, composed of poor farmers and laborers, remained illiterate.)

Egypt's largest temple complex, Karnak (pictured), was built near Thebes during the Middle Kingdom period. It consisted of four main temples, with the largest of these dedicated to the god Amun.

A new value placed on getting a proper education is reflected in a now well-known Middle Kingdom document, the *Satire of Trades*. In it, a teacher tells his pupils, "You must give yourself whole-heartedly to learning." Becoming educated, he says, will "save you from the drudgery of underlings"—that is, poor people who labor hard from sunrise to sunset. "Let me urge you to love learning more than your mother," he goes on. "There is nothing [else] like it upon Earth!"[8]

The Middle Kingdom pharaohs also enlarged the size and importance of the Egyptian army. This trend was based less on a desire to conquer other peoples and more on the perceived need to discourage would-be local troublemakers and rebels from challenging the central government. Military expansion brought with it an increased emphasis on training soldiers, erecting forts, and depicting military themes in the sculptures and paintings that decorated the royal palace. The pharaohs came to inject themselves into these depictions, building heroic images, even when not deserved. One Middle Kingdom ruler's artistic propaganda states in part, "He is vengeful when he cracks skulls, and no

The Narmer Palette

Much of the existing information about the first Egyptian pharaoh, Narmer, comes from an artifact unearthed in 1897 at Hierakonpolis, in early Egyptian times an important town on the Nile in southern Egypt. Essentially a flat plate of dark green-gray siltstone, it is routinely referred to as the "Narmer Palette." It is roughly 25 inches (64 cm) high and covered with elegant, well-preserved carvings on both sides. One side bears a striking image of Narmer wearing the crown of the White Land; the opposite side shows him with the crown of the Red Land. "The king is shown subduing his enemies, some of whom lie decapitated before him, their heads between their feet," scholar Charles Freeman writes. He continues:

> Quite apart from its historical importance, the palette shows that many conventions of Egyptian art are already in place. Status is represented by the comparative size of the figures. Narmer is the largest figure throughout. In one scene an official is shown as smaller than Narmer but still much larger than the accompanying standard-bearers. The artist is not concerned so much with providing a proper representation as with passing on detail, even if this means distorting normal perspectives. The face of the king, for instance, is shown in profile, but his eye is shown in full and the shoulders are viewed from the front [a pose today formally known as "frontalism" and informally called the "Egyptian stance"].

Charles Freeman, *Egypt, Greece, and Rome: Civilizations of the Ancient Mediterranean*. New York: Oxford University Press, 2004, p. 18.

one stands up near him." Further, he "does not allow cowardice around him," and "the bowmen retreat before him as if before the might of a great goddess."[9]

According to the reckoning of modern historians, the Middle Kingdom came to an end in about 1650 BCE when a foreign people invaded Egypt from the northeast. They are known to history as the

Hyksos. They captured Memphis and its surrounding lands, forcing the reigning pharaohs to rule from Thebes, in the south.

The New Kingdom and New Militarism

Although it took a century, the Egyptians finally defeated and expelled the Hyksos, an event that proved crucial in two ways. First, it brought the north back under the control of Egypt's native-born leaders. No less important was that those rulers now instituted a decisive shift in national policy that would profoundly shape the country's future. After the Hyksos episode, the pharaohs reasoned there was only one way they could guarantee the safety of the borders and avoid future invasions. Namely, they must go on the offensive and gain influence and control over their nearest neighbors.

In Egypt's next major era—the New Kingdom (ca. 1550–1070 BCE)—therefore, the most dominant national policies were military readiness and foreign conquest. During these centuries the pharaohs extended the country's influence far beyond its traditional borders. Accompanying the new militarism were noticeable increases in patriotism, nationalism, and artistic endeavors that doubled as propaganda. All of this created a massive base of local support for the rulers and their military exploits. "For the first time in history Egypt entered upon a path of continuing imperialism," or empire-building, stated the late historian Chester G. Starr. "The Egyptian expansion abroad appears at times in contemporary records almost as a crusade to prove the power of Egyptian civilization. In modern psychological terms it has been called a compensation for the serious blow to native pride which had come in the Hyksos conquest."[10]

> "The Egyptian expansion abroad appears at times in contemporary records almost as a crusade to prove the power of Egyptian civilization."[10]
>
> —The late scholar Chester G. Starr

A long line of New Kingdom pharaohs proved to be capable military leaders (or else were good at choosing competent generals). Amenhotep I (who reigned ca. 1525–1504 BCE), for example, expanded Egypt's already existing influence in Nubia, lying directly south of Egypt. His successor, Thutmose I (ca. 1504–1492 BCE), campaigned successfully in both Nubia and Syria. Next came Thutmose's daughter, Hatshepsut (ca. 1473–1458 BCE). She ruled at first as regent (one who rules on behalf of a minor) for her stepson, Thutmose III, who was too young to ascend the throne, and later as a pharaoh in her own right. A strong, thoughtful leader, she funded many building projects and sent traders to Punt, a little-known land lying on the Red Sea's African shores, in an effort to expand Egypt's trade and possibly its political relations.

When he finally did become pharaoh, Thutmose III (ca. 1479–1425 BCE) proved to be one of the country's most accomplished imperialists. He solidified Egyptian rule over the extensive lands stretching from the Sinai Peninsula all the way northward into central Syria. Keeping the conquered kingdoms in line provided a challenge that Thutmose met in an unusual way. Instead of stationing thousands of troops in those areas—an extremely costly approach—he took as hostages the sons of thirty-six local rulers. Afraid of losing their sons, these rulers stayed loyal to Egypt.

Egypt in Decline

Thutmose's great-grandson, Amenhotep III (ca. 1390–1352 BCE) brought the New Kingdom to its height of power and prosperity. His government operated with great efficiency, and he was an aggressive builder of temples and other major structures. Likewise, he managed the empire with skill and good judgment.

After Amenhotep's reign, however, with one notable exception, the New Kingdom pharaohs were far less effective rulers, and Egypt suffered as a result. Amenhotep's son, for instance, Amenhotep IV (ca. 1352–1336 BCE), plunged the nation into a major crisis. After changing his name to Akhenaten, the new pharaoh staged a religious revolution in which he banned the traditional gods and tried to replace them with a single deity—Aten, which he described as the blinding face of the sun. This effort failed. Most Egyptians recoiled in horror at having their cherished faith torn asunder. After Akhenaten's death, his successors restored the old gods and erased his name from as many monuments and documents as they could.

Thereafter, pharaoh after pharaoh proved weak or allowed Egypt's power and influence beyond its borders to erode. The outstanding exception—Ramesses II (ca. 1279–1213 BCE) proved to be one of the greatest leaders Egypt had ever produced. When he took the throne, the Hittites, an ambitious people from Anatolia (now Turkey), posed a serious threat to Egypt's empire in the region of Syria. In 1274 BCE, Ramesses, a gifted military leader, met the Hittites in one of the ancient era's biggest battles. The two armies, totaling some 55,000 soldiers and 4,500 chariots, clashed at Kadesh, in southern Syria. Although there was no clear winner, Ramesses halted Hittite expansion and kept the Egyptian empire intact for the moment.

Ramesses also achieved much on the domestic front. He was a prolific builder who "left behind a legacy of monuments unequalled by any other pharaoh of the New Kingdom," as the noted modern Egyptian archaeologist Zahi Hawass puts it. "No site in Egypt was untouched by his builders and his monuments. His temples, chapels, statues, and stelae can be found throughout the country."[11]

Ramesses II leads his troops against the war lions of the Hittite army in 1274 BCE. The battle produced no clear victor but it resulted in a halt to Hittite expansion efforts—at least for a while.

The Great Hymn to Aten

Multiple versions of a magnificent hymn to the pharaoh Akhenaten's sole god, Aten, were discovered in the tombs of some of his chief courtiers. Most historians think that the so-called maverick pharaoh composed the sacred song himself. It lavished praise on Aten, calling him the world's creator and crediting him with fashioning humans, animals, and plants. The tone of this writing suggests that Akhenaten and his fellow worshipers felt genuine, almost ecstatic love and joy for the god, whom they envisioned as the sun's glowing disk. One of the several passages reads:

> Splendid you rise, O living Aten, eternal lord! You are radiant, beauteous, mighty; your love is great, immense; your rays light up all faces; your bright hue gives light to hearts when you fill the Two Lands [of Egypt] with your love. [You are an] august god who fashioned himself, who made every land, created what is in it; all peoples, herds, and flocks, all trees that grow from soil. . . . Your rays light the whole earth; every heart acclaims your sight when you are risen as their lord! When you set in [the] sky's western light-land, they lie down as if to die, their heads covered, their noses stopped, until you dawn in [the] sky's eastern light-land. Their arms adore your *ka* [soul], as you nourish the hearts by your beauty. One lives when you cast your rays. Every land is in festivity.

Quoted in Miriam Lichtheim, ed., *Ancient Egyptian Literature: A Book of Readings*, vol. 2. Berkeley: University of California Press, 2006, pp. 91–92.

None of Ramesses's successors came close to equaling his accomplishments. After his passing, the New Kingdom rapidly declined and Egypt lost most of its empire. In the next few centuries, periods of disunity like the one that had ended the Old Kingdom wracked the country, and a number of weak foreign-born kings sat on its throne. Even worse, in 674 BCE the warlike Assyrians (from Mesopotamia) invaded, causing much death and misery. Similarly, in 525 BCE the

Persians (from Iran) attacked and seized control of Egypt, which became a province of the Persian Empire.

Alive in People's Imaginations

Thereafter, for many long centuries Egypt remained under the control of foreign rulers or empires. In 332 BCE, the Macedonian-Greek conqueror Alexander III, later called "the Great," entered the country. The locals thought he was liberating them from the Persians, but the reality was that their Persian oppressors had simply been replaced by Greek ones. In the years following Alexander's death in 323 BCE, one of his followers, Ptolemy, seized the Egyptian throne and instituted a Greek family line of rulers—the Ptolemaic dynasty. It was destined to endure for nearly three centuries.

Under the Ptolemaic pharaohs, Egypt further declined, becoming a pale shadow of the powerful nation and empire it had once been. During these years the Romans (masters of the Italian peninsula) subjugated all the Greek kingdoms and city-states in the eastern Mediterranean sphere except for Ptolemaic Egypt, which they tolerated for a time. Egypt's largely impotent leaders could do little more than wait and hope for the best.

Finally, they too succumbed to the reality of Roman military and political superiority. In 51 BCE, the last of the Ptolemies, as well as the last independent pharaoh—Cleopatra VII—ascended Egypt's throne. On the positive side, she was highly intelligent, talented, and ambitious; indeed, in an earlier age she might have been one of the country's greatest rulers. But in the world she was born into, Rome's mastery was close to inevitable. In 31 BCE, Cleopatra and her Roman ally and lover, Marcus Antonius (now better known as Mark Antony), met disastrous defeat at Actium, in western Greece. The lovers took their own lives the following year. Then the victor—the future first Roman emperor, Augustus—made Egypt a Roman province, which it remained for the rest of the ancient period.

> "The civilization of the pharaohs is alive and well in the imaginations of people the world over."[12]
>
> —Historian Toby Wilkinson

In this way, as historian Toby Wilkinson says, "the proud three-thousand-year-old tradition of pharaonic independence was snuffed out, once and for all." Yet even mighty Rome could not erase the memory of that colorful, compelling tradition. Over time, Wilkinson asserts, "ancient Egypt as a concept and an ideal" managed to survive the ages and prosper. He continues:

> The rulers of the Nile Valley and their hard-pressed subjects succeeded in creating a uniquely powerful culture, one that has fascinated and bewitched all who have come into contact with it. [Today] in film and literature, and through architecture, design, and tourism, the civilization of the pharaohs is alive and well in the imaginations of people the world over. The ancient Egyptians could not have wished for more.[12]

CHAPTER TWO

How Did the Nile River Make Egyptian Civilization Possible?

Focus Questions

1. In what ways did the Nile River sustain life for the ancient Egyptians? Which of these mattered most and why?
2. What kind of society might have developed in ancient Egypt without the annual flooding of the Nile River? Explain your thinking.
3. How important are art and leisure activities to the development of a civilization—and why?

Modern historians are unanimous in pointing out that the four so-called cradles of civilization—in Mesopotamia, India, China, and Egypt—all grew up along and depended on the life-giving waters of major rivers. The winding waterway that sustained the Egyptians was the world's longest river, the mighty Nile. Its source lies in the highlands of east-central Africa and from there it meanders for more than 4,130 miles (6,647 km) northward to its delta in northern Egypt. That wide, phenomenally fertile area where the river empties into the Mediterranean Sea is shaped like half of a giant pie.

If one could magically look down from high above at that half a pie and the rest of ancient Egypt, one would see a vertical, very narrow greenish-colored ribbon attached to the delta. Dividing Egypt roughly in half, that slender band measured only 4 to 13 miles (6 to 21 km) wide in most places. It was made up of the river itself plus the well-watered lands lying directly along its banks. With the exception of a handful of tiny, scattered oases, the delta and green ribbon were the only parts of Egypt capable of sustaining large numbers of people. The remainder of the country was desert.

"Without the waters and fertile flood-plain of the Nile, it is highly unlikely that Egyptian civilization would have developed in the deserts of northeastern Africa."[13]

—Egyptologist Ian Shaw

As a result most Egyptians lived on farms or in villages or towns situated along the Nile. They employed its waters to irrigate their fields, to drink, to bathe and play in, and, using small boats, to travel and transport goods on. Clearly, if the Nile had not formed where it did, large numbers of people could not and would not have settled in Egypt's otherwise arid wastelands. As noted Egyptologist Ian Shaw says, "Without the waters and fertile flood-plain of the Nile, it is highly unlikely that Egyptian civilization would have developed in the deserts of northeastern Africa."[13]

The Gift of the River

That ancient civilization remained on a relatively small scale for many centuries. This was because the early settlers of the Nile Valley did not know how to properly use the Nile's annual floods—which they came to call the "inundation." These yearly natural events furnished them with both water and fresh soil, as archaeologist Charles Gates explains:

> Swelling from spring rains in central Africa and the Ethiopian highlands, the river becomes rich with silt washed from the hills. Gradually the water and silt travel northward, reaching Egypt a few months later. Egypt saw the Nile at its lowest in May, but then the river would rise until mid-August when it spilled over its banks into the adjacent fields. For two months the farmland lay buried beneath the floodwaters. Then in October the river receded, flushing away noxious salts and leaving behind a new layer of rich, fertile soil.[14]

Harnessing the inundation made it possible to practice agriculture on a much larger scale than before, so over time Egypt's population significantly increased. In fact, it eventually became possible to feed millions of people. Modern scholars estimate that ancient Egypt's

Women wash clothing in the Nile River and fill vessels with water to be used in their homes and villages. The Nile provided precious water for various needs including irrigation, drinking, cooking, bathing, and transport.

population reached an all-time high of 5 million to 7 million in the late first millennium BCE.

This was, more or less, the culture that Herodotus witnessed when he visited Egypt in the 400s BCE. In a now famous remark, he called that culture the "gift of the river," pointedly crediting the Nile with making Egyptian civilization possible. His full statement, from his *Histories*, reads: "It is clear to any intelligent observer, even if he has no previous information on the subject, that the Egypt to which we sail nowadays is, as it were, the gift of the river."[15]

Traditional Farming Methods

Although that gift entailed the river aiding and nourishing the Egyptians in all manner of ways, by far the most critical of these was creating a large, dependable food source for the country's considerable population. Indeed, whether they were rich or poor, everyone had to eat. Moreover, food was often a form of currency. People used it to pay someone for his or her work, traded it for items of equal value (the barter system), and even paid their taxes with it. So farming, which produced the food, was crucial to maintaining both life and many facets of the everyday social order. For these and other reasons, agriculture remained always the mainstay of Egypt's economy throughout the ancient era.

Modern scholars know a fair amount about ancient Egyptian farmers and the methods they employed. In part this is because ancient artists depicted diverse aspects of planting and harvesting in tomb paintings. In addition, numerous agricultural tools and practices used in ancient Egypt survived into medieval and modern times in several sectors of the Middle East.

Using simple wooden plows drawn by cattle, farmers sow seeds in their fields. In some instances, where soil was especially fertile, farmers could spread their seeds without even needing to plow.

Planting is an instructive example. Egyptian farmers used simple wooden plows drawn by cattle or donkeys to create furrows in the soil. In particularly fertile spots, they did not even bother to plow, but instead simply spread their seeds and walked some goats or pigs across the field to work them in. The scattering of the seeds was done by hand, from a seed-filled sack worn around the neck.

After the fall planting season, while the crops were growing, many farmers made a little extra income by doing craft work. Others labored temporarily on large construction projects sponsored by the government. When it was time to harvest the crops in the spring, farmers once more relied on traditional methods. One was to use sharpened wooden sickles to cut down the mature plants. Typically, a farmer, his male relatives, and when possible some hired hands lined up and walked through the crops, swinging their sickles as they went. The women and children of the family followed in a second line, scooping up the downed plants and loading them into wicker baskets.

In the cases of barley and wheat, next came the threshing process, in which the grains themselves were separated from the stalks. Often a farmer and his helpers spread the harvested grain on some flat stones and had donkeys or oxen trample it. While this was happening, the workers commonly sang traditional songs. Among the most popular were verses from "The Hymn to Hapy," god of the inundation and through it bringer of food and prosperity. "Songs of the harp are made for you," one verse begins, continuing:

> One sings to you with clapping hands. The youths, your children, hail you, crowds adorn themselves for you, who comes with riches, decks the land, makes every human body flourish. [Hapy] sustains the pregnant woman's heart, and loves a multitude of herds. When he rises at the residence, men feast on the meadow's gifts![16]

Bathing, Cooking, and More

Although making agriculture possible was perhaps the Nile's prime gift to the Egyptians, the river gave them much more. Its waters also kept them clean, for example. Abundant evidence shows that, as a people, the Egyptians were extremely concerned with physical cleanliness; hence, they washed several times a day. Some people bathed in the river itself. Among the surviving references to this custom, the most familiar is from the biblical book of Exodus. "Now the daughter of Pharaoh," it reads, "came down to bathe at the river, and her maidens walked beside the river."[17]

Most Egyptians lacked the time to get to the river as often as needed to stay clean, however, so they gave themselves what today is called a sponge bath. Most often the water for this ritual came from the Nile (although some came from ponds and canals, of which the latter were fed by the river). Each morning a family's women made one or two trips to the river to fetch water, which they carried in pottery jars that they balanced on their heads.

Reaching home, German historian Eugen Strouhal explains, the women poured the water "into the huge ceramic vessels standing by the doorways or in the courtyards of every house." Residents dipped into these big water jars not only for personal washing, but also for drinking, cooking, washing dishes, and doing laundry. "Only small items of clothing," Strouhal adds, "were washed at home. For the 'big wash,' women went to the source of the water [the river] and did the job as a pleasant social event."[18]

Their Homes in the Water

As vital as the Nile's water was to an average Egyptian on a daily basis, the creatures that made their homes in that water were of nearly equal value. The river supported numerous kinds of fish, including catfish, eel, and perch. (Modern studies of ancient tomb paintings depicting fishermen at work have identified more than twenty Nile fish species.) All through the ancient era fishing was an economic necessity for most of the poor Egyptians who lived in marshes near the river and did not farm for a living.

One of the most common techniques these fishermen employed was to stand up in a boat and jab a long, sharpened spear at the fish as they swam by. Also widespread was the use of a rod and line quite similar to the kind used in modern fishing. The hooks that ancient Egyptian anglers used were initially made from bone carved into the desired shape, but over time they learned to fashion their hooks from copper and bronze.

Singing the River's Praises

The Nile's life-giving properties were so important to the Egyptians that they often endowed that river with godlike status. In the early second millennium BCE a special hymn dedicated to the river developed. People sang it during a yearly religious festival that celebrated the inundation, the gentle flood that provided both water for irrigation and a new layer of rich soil. The hymn stated in part,

> Praise to you, O Nile, that issues forth from the earth and comes to nourish the dwellers in Egypt. Secret of movement. A darkness in the daytime. That waters the meadows that [the sun god] Ra has created to nourish all cattle, that gives drink to the desert places that are far from water. His dew it is that falls from heaven. [O Nile you are] beloved of the earth-god, controller of the corn-god who makes every workshop of [the god] Ptah to flourish. Lord of fish that makes the water fowl to go upstream, without a bird falling. That makes barley and creates wheat, that makes the temples to keep festival. If he [the Nile] is sluggish, the nostrils are stopped up, and all men are brought low. [He is a] bringer of nourishment, plenteous of sustenance, creating all things good. Lord of reverence, sweet of savior, appeasing evil, [while] filling the barns and widening the granaries, and giving to the poor. Causing trees to grow according to the utmost desire, so that men go not in lack of them!

Quoted in W.K. Simpson, ed., *The Literature of Ancient Egypt: An Anthology of Stories, Instructions, and Poetry*. New Haven, CT: Yale University Press, 2003, p. 96.

Egyptian fishermen also developed more complex methods of catching fish. One was to fashion traps from the stems of river reeds, which they interwove into basketlike contraptions. Typically, a fisherman weighted the trap, attached a thin rope to it, and lowered it to the bottom of the river or a canal. Then, to make sure he would later remember where the trap was, he marked the spot with a buoy composed of a type of wood light enough to float. A sculpted panel found in the tomb of a well-to-do Egyptian depicts two fishermen using just such a trap. In a caption carved into the panel, one man says, "Pull hard on the oars so that we can get on top of [the fish]!" After he has raised the trap, the other man calls out, "Full to the brim! This time we've done it!"[19]

Still another ancient Egyptian fishing technique, one still fairly common around the globe today, involved the use of large nets. Tomb sculptures show fishermen fastening stone, clay, and metal weights to one edge of a net so that that part would sink down to the river bottom. While using wooden floats to maintain the opposite edge of the net on the surface, men sitting in two boats dragged the net along while their colleagues rowed. Any fish that happened to be in the area between the boats were snared.

Lurking River Dangers

The fishing methods described so far were handed down through the generations and continue in regular use in Egypt and many other lands today. Certain dangers that ancient Egyptian anglers faced also remain in effect within the Nile itself. One of these threats is a catfish—the *Malapterurus*—that weighs up to 40 pounds (18 kg) and delivers an electric shock that can knock over an adult man. That scary creature, which even Nile crocodiles try to avoid, is pictured prominently on the famous Narmer Palette, a surviving artifact celebrating Egypt's first pharaoh.

Meanwhile, those river crocodiles regularly lurked, waiting to attack birds, fishermen, bathers, and other unwary animals and humans who wandered too close. A surviving early second-millennium BCE document tells of a fisherman who made this unfortunate mistake. "His work takes him to a river infested with crocodiles," it states. "When the time comes to count up [the day's catch], he wrings his hands over it, without even thinking that there might be a crocodile around! Too late he is gripped with fear. Then as soon as he reaches the water he falls [to the crocodile] as if struck by the hand of god."[20]

> "His work takes him to a river infested with crocodiles."[20]
>
> —A surviving ancient Egyptian document

In addition, fishermen, and many other people as well, were careful to follow various ancient religious rules involving fish and other river

A model found in an ancient tomb in Thebes depicts fishermen in two boats dragging a net between them to obtain their daily catch. This and other fishing methods were passed on from generation to generation.

wildlife. Some of these creatures were seen as divinely protected, and not to be killed for any reason. One reason for this unusual attitude was widespread literal belief in the then well-known myth of Osiris. In that story the evil god Seth sliced up the body of the virtuous deity Osiris and tossed some of the pieces in the Nile, where fish and other animals ate them. One kind of fish that did so was the Oxyrhynchus. Because many people thought it carried some of Osiris's own flesh inside it, they equated killing the fish with attacking Osiris himself—an unforgivable crime.

Swimmers, Jousters, and Daredevils

The Nile also served as a venue for numerous sports and leisure activities in ancient Egypt. Evidence suggests that swimming in the river was widely popular, for example, and further that a majority of the country's residents could swim. In fact, the special picture-language employed by literate Egyptians—hieroglyphics—had a specific symbol that stood for swimming. Also, beginning in the mid-second millennium BCE craftsmen created finely carved artifacts that frequently depicted people swimming. An excellent example can be seen at New

When the subject of ancient Egyptian farming comes up, most people envision stalwart farmers planting and harvesting crops in the rich soil laid down each year in the Nile's inundation. Although this image is accurate, it is important to point out that many Egyptian farmers were also ranchers who raised livestock, sometimes in large numbers. The late historian Lionel Casson summarized ranching along the ancient Nile, saying that the larger ranches raised "sizable herds of cattle." Near the end of the New Kingdom, he goes on, the farms run by the temple of the god Amun

> owned more than four hundred thousand head. One of the herds, in the eastern part of the delta, was so large that almost a thousand men were needed to handle it. Cattle rustling seems to have been as much a problem in ancient Egypt as in the American West, and the same means were used to combat it—branding. The ranch hands herded the animals into a corner of a field, lassoed each in turn, rolled it onto its back with its feet trussed [bound], and branded it on the right shoulder—with the inevitable scribe nearby to keep track of the inventory figures. Great care and attention were given to fattening the herds, much more than to the herdsmen. In one [surviving painting], the artist, with typically sardonic Egyptian humor, shows a row of beefy cattle led by a herdsman so scrawny that every bone in his body sticks out!

Lionel Casson, *Daily Life in Ancient Egypt*. New York: American Heritage, 1994, pp. 39–40.

York's Metropolitan Museum of Art. It consists of an elegant cosmetic spoon (for applying make-up) from the reign of one of that period's most important pharaohs—Amenhotep III. The spoon's handle is shaped like a nude swimming woman.

Other popular water sports among the Egyptians involved boats moving on the Nile or through the irrigation canals that flowed off of it. For instance, the pharaohs, their officials, and other members of the upper classes regularly held races featuring riverboats propelled by rowers. Meanwhile, ordinary people took part in what some modern experts call "water-jousting." This rough-and-tumble sport employed small and light but sturdy vessels crafted from bundled plant stems. Apparently as few as two and as many as dozens of boats could take part. Each held a crew that included one or more sitting rowers and one standing "warrior" who brandished a long stick. As the boats engaged one another, trying to gain some sort of advantage, the standing men swung their sticks, attempting to knock their opponents into the water. The last vessel with a warrior still standing was the winner.

Although water-jousting could be aggressive and probably caused some injuries, it was not nearly as dangerous as shooting the Nile's rapids. A series of rapids exist at the river's cataracts, spots where the ground level changes height, causing the water to form abnormally turbulent currents and waves. The first-century CE Roman playwright Seneca the Younger owned a house in Egypt when it was a Roman province. He described a cataract he witnessed as "a remarkable spectacle" where the river "surges through rocks which are steep and jagged in many places." There, he went on, the Nile shows its power "in a violent torrent that leaps forward through narrow passages [and] finally struggles through the obstructions in its way. Then, suddenly losing its support, [the water] falls down an enormous depth with a tremendous crash that echoes through the surrounding regions."[21]

"They are violently tossed about in the raging rapids [until] they reach the narrowest channels, [where they] are swept along by the whole force of the river."[22]

—Ancient Roman playwright Seneca the Younger

Seneca frequently observed young Egyptian men daringly rowing right into those rapids. He recorded one such scene in writing, saying that the daredevils

embark on small boats, two to a boat, and one rows while the other bails out water. Then they are violently tossed about in the raging rapids [until] they reach the narrowest channels, [where they] are swept along by the whole force of the river.

They control the rushing boat by hand and plunge head downward to the great terror of the onlookers. You would believe sorrowfully that by now they were drowned and overwhelmed by such a mass of water, when far from the place where they fell, they shoot out as from a catapult, still sailing, and the subsiding wave does not submerge them, but carries them on to smooth waters.[22]

Whether in supplying water for growing crops, drinking, and bathing, or in providing food and a setting for leisure and relaxation, the Nile was in a very real sense the lifeblood of ancient Egypt. As the late historian Lionel Casson fittingly put it, even today "the great river" makes civilization possible in the region. It "creates in the midst of sterility an elongated oasis that from prehistoric times gave not merely life, but a good life, to the Egypt of the pharaohs."[23]

CHAPTER THREE

How Did an Agrarian Society Build Some of the World's Most Enduring Structures?

Focus Questions

1. What importance did the pyramids have in ancient Egyptian culture?
2. Which building techniques do you think were the most innovative for the time period? Explain your thinking.
3. Do you think disagreements between scientists, historians, and other types of researchers are a benefit or detriment to efforts to expand knowledge? Explain your answer.

From a flat, sandy plain not far from Egypt's capital city, Cairo, three enormous stone structures soar high into the air. They are the world-renowned pyramids of Giza, the name of the plateau on which they rest. Three pharaohs of the Old Kingdom—Khufu, Khafre, and Menkaura—erected them some forty-six centuries ago to serve as their tombs.

Particularly impressive is the largest of the three massive monuments, Khufu's final resting place. When first built it measured 481 feet (147 m) tall, almost three times the height of New York's Statue of Liberty. That made it the tallest human-made structure in the world, a distinction it held through the ages until France's Eiffel Tower surpassed it in 1889. Moreover, Khafre's pyramid is only slightly smaller than Khufu's.

The sheer size of these edifices is not the only thing that people find compelling about them. Beginning in the late ancient era, throughout the Middle Ages that followed, and even well into modern times, an air of mystery surrounded them. Many of the travelers who gazed at them in awe asked certain often-repeated, rather pointed questions. Chief among them are: "Exactly who built the Giza structures and Egypt's numerous other pyramid-tombs?" and "How did they manage to do it?"

It turns out that these queries are closely related. Archaeologists and other scholars have determined that the once widely accepted idea that slaves erected the pyramids is incorrect. Rather, they were built primarily by free Egyptian farmers.

Evidence also shows that these workers had no advanced tools, not even the simple block and tackle (a combination of pulleys and ropes used for lifting). Indeed, with the exception of a few knives and saws made from copper—a soft metal almost useless for such large-scale building—they employed picks, axes, chisels, and knives made of stone. The overriding question therefore becomes: What knowledge and methods allowed a society of agrarians, or farmers, who were armed only with primitive tools, to create the mighty pyramid-tombs?

Reporting for Duty at Giza

In exploring how ancient Egyptian farmers managed to build the great pyramids at Giza, the logical place to begin is with the farmers themselves. Many people today might find it odd that individuals who grew up on farms and raised crops and livestock sometimes doubled as construction workers. In ancient Egypt, however, that sort of situation was fairly common. Large numbers of farmers had a few idle months at their disposal between planting and harvesting. The pharaoh and his officials were well aware of that fact. Frequently needing thousands of cheap laborers to help construct temples, palaces, and other large structures, the government regularly offered farmers a deal that was hard to turn down. In exchange for doing the needed labor, they would eliminate some or all of their tax obligations.

This is how thousands of farmers ended up working on Khufu's and Khafre's giant tombs. When it was time for them to report for duty at Giza, almost overnight the normally sparsely inhabited plateau became extremely crowded. Modern estimates for the number of workers involved range from five thousand to more than twenty thousand. To accommodate all those people, a new town sprang up

The pyramids of Giza rise from the desert floor. They are fascinating for many reasons, but in particular because it is astounding that such enormous structures could have been built by an agrarian society.

at Giza courtesy of the central government. The officials in charge of the project knew that only a handful of the workers lived close enough to commute from and to their homes each day. So thousands of small dwellings had to be built on the plateau to house the bulk of the workforce.

The existence of that workers' town was unknown until the 1990s. It was discovered by a joint Egyptian-American team of excavators headed by Egypt's leading archaeologist, Zahi Hawass, and American Egyptologist Mark Lehner. Describing this significant find, Hawass later stated,

> During the construction of the sewage system [near] the great pyramid, we found a large Old Kingdom settlement about 3 km [1.8 miles] square. We recorded a continuous layer of mud-brick buildings starting about 165 feet [50 m] south of the valley temple of Khufu and extending about 1 mile [1.6 km] to

the south. Among the artifacts [excavated] are thousands of fragments of every day pottery and bread molds, cooking pots, beer jars, and trays for sifting grain and flour. . . . I believe that there were two types of settlement, one for the workmen who moved the stones, and the other camp for the artisans [who dressed the stones].[24]

In addition, fairly close to the workers' town, Hawass and Lehner uncovered a cemetery containing numerous tombs of those laborers. These graves were small and modest compared to Khufu's and Khafre's vast tombs that towered nearby. A typical worker's grave consisted of a hole dug in the sand and lined with some mud bricks. Sometimes the dead person's relatives placed a small stone grave marker atop the hole.

The diggers found a treasure trove of artifacts inside the graves as well, which have revealed a great deal about the workers and their lives. Among those objects are small carved figurines of the male workers and their family members. One figurine, Hawass explains, "depicts a woman seated on a backless chair with her hands on her knees. An inscription on the chair identifies her as Hepeny-kawes. She wears a black wig with hair parted in the middle and reaching to her shoulders." Another carved figure resting in the same grave depicts her husband, a man named Kaihep. Other grave goods, Hawass continues, show "that males and females were equally represented, mostly buried in fetal positions, with face to the east and head to the north. Many of the men died between the ages of 30 and 35. Below the age of 30, a higher mortality was found in females [likely] reflecting the hazards of childbirth."[25]

> "I believe that there were two types of settlement, one for the workmen who moved the stones, and the other camp for the artisans [who dressed the stones]."[24]
>
> —Egyptian archaeologist Zahi Hawass

Moving the Initial Stones

The farmer-workers, some of whom left behind those grave markers, performed a variety of tasks during the construction of the pharaohs' massive tombs. These hulking structures were made mostly by stack-

A figurine of a woman kneading dough dates to Egypt's Old Kingdom period. Figurines like this one present a realistic picture of daily life among the people who built and lived beside the pyramids.

ing huge numbers of big, heavy stone blocks on top of one another. Hawass, Lehner, and other experts estimate that Khufu's pyramid is composed of more than 2.3 million separate stones, each weighing, on average, two and a half tons.

One crucial task was to quarry those stones, which kept at least several hundred workers constantly busy. Other laborers transported the blocks to the work site on the plateau. How people who lacked backhoes, metal cranes, trucks, trains, and other modern lifting and

A Compromise Approach

Some modern experts favor the idea of debris ramps to explain how Egyptian pyramid-builders raised the stone blocks to higher and higher levels. Others, Peter Hodges prominent among them, think the workers used levers in one way or another to accomplish the same task. There are also scholars who think that *both* methods may have been used on a single construction project. One expert who supported this compromise approach was the late French archaeologist Jean-Philippe Lauer (1902–2001). He argued that the builders of Khufu's pyramid erected ramps of varying sizes and shapes. At the same time, he said, lifting methods using levers and ropes would have been useful for certain specialized jobs. Regarding the ramps, Lauer reasoned that the workers created four large ones—one on each of the structure's four sides. In addition he proposed that a fifth ramp ran from the pyramid to the main Giza stone quarry. As the giant tomb grew taller, he said, the builders would have extended that fifth ramp in order to reach the progressively higher courses. Meanwhile, he contended, the task of constructing the pharaoh's burial chambers in the structure's center required installing several smaller earthen or debris ramps on the exposed courses of the half-built pyramid. Finally, he said, the workers faced the difficult job of lifting the stone blocks making up the structure's topmost courses. In his opinion, they may have achieved this by devising a clever system of levers, beams, ropes, and counterweights.

transporting devices were able to move such heavy objects from one place to another has fascinated generations of academics and travelers.

The answer is that they did it using a combination of ingenuity and raw muscle power. First, members of a work gang placed a sledge—essentially a large wooden sled—beside a stone they desired to move. Then some of the men grasped sturdy wooden levers and jammed them into the dirt beneath one side of the block. Allotting several individuals to each lever, they next pulled down on these beams with all their might. This tilted the stone up just enough so that several more men could slip one side of the sledge into the small gap the levers had created. Bit by bit, the gang members used the levers and their bodily strength to nudge the stone completely onto the sledge.

Finally, the workers attached ropes to the sledge and dragged it across the sands. When possible they made the job easier by pulling it over a bed of wooden rollers. Some members of the gang picked up the rollers the sledge had already passed over, carried them around the slow-moving object, and laid them down in front of it. As University of Cambridge scholar Kate Spence points out, sometimes the rollers were laid down as a semipermanent floor of the roadway leading to large buildings under construction. Such a roadway excavated at Lisht, some 30 miles (48 km) south of Cairo, she says, "was found to consist of a series of smooth timbers set into a solid mud runway. Such a track would considerably reduce friction and aid the passage of the sledges."[26]

When the initial stones reached the Giza construction site, they went into creating the pyramid's base, or foundation, which measured a whopping 756 feet (230 m) on each side. In all, the base covered some 13.6 acres (5.5 ha), approximately equivalent to nine football fields. Once those lowest blocks were in place, the workers began stacking more of them in layers, which experts refer to as courses.

One obvious problem is that lifting the tremendously heavy stones became more and more difficult as the courses grew higher. Today, builders deal with such problems by employing sophisticated cranes, electric elevators, and other advanced lifting techniques. But the ancient Egyptians possessed none of those fruits of modern science.

The Debate over Ramps

Therein lies the ongoing mystery concerning raising the great pyramids. Modern scholars can describe with near certainty all the steps in that overall process *except* for the exact manner in which the workers lifted the stones up to form the increasingly higher courses. Experts have put forward a number of proposals to explain it over the past century and a half and still debate them.

The most widely accepted theory, at least until recently, was that the pyramid-builders used ramps to lift the stones upward. Today, however, engineers have pointed out that wooden ramps, even very strong ones, would have worked only for the first few courses. As the later courses continued to rise, such ramps would have needed to rapidly become

Workers use a sledge to drag hefty stone blocks across the desert to the pyramid-building site. Sometimes they placed a bed of wooden rollers beneath the sledge, creating a track that made the job a little easier.

longer, thicker, and heavier. Soon they would have been so big and weighty as to be impossible to construct and move.

For that reason various scholars have suggested that the workers fashioned large-scale earthen ramps. This could have been done by piling up mammoth mounds of dirt and sand mixed with small shards of limestone and other stone debris. An entire side of the growing structure could have been buried and hidden by such a ramp, which might well have eventually stretched hundreds of feet away from the pyramid. Then when the topmost courses of stone blocks had been laid, the workers could have torn down the ramp and carted away the debris. One piece of evidence supporting this theory is that archaeologists have discovered large amounts of that type of debris in the ancient remains of a stone quarry on the Giza plateau. The stuff could well be what is left of a ramp or ramps used to erect Khufu's or Khafre's tombs.

Another area of uncertainty among the experts is how such ramps were shaped, as several workable arrangements are feasible. It is also possible that no regular or typical approach was used. Rather, some scholars think that some pyramid-builders used debris ramps of a certain shape, whereas others employed differently shaped ones. In a similar vein it has been suggested that the builders of Khufu's pyramid used debris ramps having two or more different shapes, depending on which worked best at a given stage of the construction process.

One probable ramp configuration used during the building of Khufu's tomb is a straight version installed at a right angle to one of the structure's four sides. This would have worked well enough for the courses of stones in the pyramid's lower third. But in order to add the next courses above them, a ramp of that shape would have needed to be so long and massive it would have taken nearly as long to erect as the pyramid itself.

Other feasible debris ramps could conceivably have been employed in the creation of Khufu's gigantic tomb. One is a spiral type that might have twisted around three or all four of the building's sides. Another possible ramp shape is one that zigzags, running back and forth along one side; still another version is a cluster of straight ramps on each of the four sides. Kate Spence thinks the last of these approaches was most likely used for installing most of the upper courses of Khufu's pyramid. "It seems likely that different solutions for raising blocks were used as the project progressed," she says. She continues:

> "During construction of the lower courses, many small ramps may have ensured a high flow rate of blocks to the working levels."[27]
>
> —Scholar Kate Spence

Approximately 96 percent of the volume of a pyramid is in its bottom two-thirds, and during construction of the lower courses, many small ramps may have ensured a high flow rate of blocks to the working levels. Towards the summit of the pyramid the flow rate would have been slower to allow for the difficulty of raising the blocks, and at the very top a considerable amount of improvisation would have been necessary to lift and position the blocks.[27]

A More Recent Theory

Large ramps made of sand and debris remain a viable explanation for how the Egyptians, with their primitive technology, were able to raise such heavy stones to great heights. However, a more recent theory suggested by English master builder Peter Hodges has gained considerable ground with leading scholars. He proposes that much or most of the heavy lifting was accomplished using levers in an unusual way.

To reach that conclusion, Hodges and some helpers performed experiments using two-ton stone blocks quite similar to those making up Khufu's and Khafre's pyramids. A mere two of the helpers managed to lever up one end of a block. At that moment they jammed some wooden wedges into the open space they had created; next they repeated that process on the block's opposite side. In only a few minutes, they were able to lift the block up several inches. Guided by Hodges, the two helpers continued the procedure until

Pyramidal Height: Real and Perceived

Whatever exact construction methods the builders of Khufu's and Khafre's pyramids employed, the goal was to create what were then the world's largest structures. They achieved that goal, to be sure. However, for millennia to come, people argued about which of the two towering tombs was actually the biggest. This debate was fueled by various technical factors that made determining that fact difficult. Strictly from the standpoint of simple measurement, Khufu's pyramid was always the larger of the two. Called by the Egyptians *Akhet-Khufu*, or "Khufu's Horizon," it was initially 481 feet (147 m) tall. In comparison, Khafre's pyramid measured 448 feet (137 m) in height. But over time scavengers removed several of the outer casing stones near the summit of Khufu's tomb to use in constructing buildings in nearby Cairo. The structure thereby lost about 30 feet (9 m) of its original height. By contrast, many of the original upper casing stones on Khafre's tomb remained intact. As a result of these factors, Khafre's pyramid came to look somewhat taller. Adding to this perception is an illusion created by that structure's placement on the plateau. Khafre's tomb was built on a slightly higher level of the underlying bedrock than Khufu's was—to be exact, 33 feet (10 m) higher. This fact has long given people standing nearby the false impression that Khafre's pyramid is taller than Khufu's.

they had raised the stone as high as an average course in Khufu's pyramid.

If Hodges is correct, dozens, or maybe hundreds, of similar two-person teams employed this technique day in and day out, raising the stone courses a bit at a time. One of the more attractive aspects of this lever method, researcher Robert M. Schoch points out, "is that it eliminates ramps or scaffolding. The pyramid itself becomes the platform on which the men work as they raise the stone blocks from one level to the next. When they put the last stone in place, they simply pack up their tools and go home. There was no ancillary [secondary] structure to remove."[28]

Another reason why numerous scholars find Hodges's theory convincing is that it closely resembles the lifting method Herodotus described after speaking with local Egyptians during his visit to their land. "When the base was complete," he wrote, "the blocks for the first tier above it were lifted from the ground level by devices made of short timbers." Another team of workers "raised the blocks a stage higher, then yet another which raised them higher still. Each tier, or story, had its set of levers."[29]

Whether the pyramid-builders used large debris ramps or teams of workers employing levers, either way the method they employed to lift millions of extremely heavy stones was quite simple. It involved no advanced or complex technology. Rather, it required just a dose of dogged determination, a lot of physical exertion, and of course considerable amounts of time. This explains how some mainly poor and illiterate ancient farmers who lacked advanced technology were able to construct some of the largest and most enduring structures in human history.

> "The pyramid itself becomes the platform on which the men work as they raise the stone blocks from one level to the next."[28]
>
> —Researcher Robert M. Schoch

CHAPTER FOUR

How Did Religious Beliefs Shape Egyptian Views of Life and Death?

Focus Questions

1. What aspects of everyday life and thought in ancient Egypt were most influenced by religious beliefs—and in what ways?
2. Why did so many important Egyptian deities take the shape of animals?
3. Do you think a polytheistic society, meaning one that believes in many gods, would develop different values than a monotheistic society, meaning one that believes in a single god? Using examples, explain your answer.

After his visit to Egypt in the fifth-century BCE, the Greek historian and traveler Herodotus remarked about the natives' incredibly high degree of religious devotion. His actual words were, "They are religious to excess, beyond any other nation in the world." He then went on to give examples of their intense piety. Out of deep respect for their multiple gods, he said, they "wear linen clothes which they make a special point of continually washing." Equating cleanliness with godliness, they preferred "to be clean rather than good-looking,"[30] he added. Next he launched into a long and detailed description of Egyptian priests, their dedication to the gods, and their fascinating personal customs.

Surviving comments by other ancient historians confirm that Herodotus did not exaggerate about how important religion was to the Egyptians. It was not only that they strongly believed in the existence of the gods and took comfort from that belief, but their religious devotion also had a direct bearing on the way they saw themselves, the universe, and their place within the divinely run cosmic order.

On the one hand, religious beliefs shaped the Egyptians' views of their earthly lives. This included the areas of social customs, morality, treatment of both fellow humans and animals, and in general how civilized people should act in the world. On the other, religious beliefs profoundly affected the way an Egyptian visualized death and the afterlife and prepared to one day enter that mysterious post-life realm.

> "They are religious to excess, beyond any other nation in the world."[30]
>
> —Fifth-century BCE Greek historian Herodotus

Natural Forces and the Divine

The sources of these strong religious beliefs that had such a powerful bearing on how the Egyptians perceived both life and death lie deeply shrouded in the country's prehistoric past. Long before the first pharaoh, Narmer, established the Egyptian nation, the residents of the Nile Valley had come to recognize a large group of gods. Each of these deities had its personal niche in the natural, or cosmic, order.

Indeed, most often these divinities were directly associated with natural forces and phenomena. They included the warmth of the sun, rain and storms, floods and other natural disasters, the behaviors of various animals, the moon's phases and monthly movements, and recognizable patterns of stars in the night sky. The earliest Egyptians assumed that these phenomena were controlled by the gods and directly connected to earthly life. Egyptologist Rosalie David explains that once people had settled down permanently in the Nile Valley, their

> earliest concepts and religious beliefs and experiences developed. They were always aware of their environment and of the impact of the natural forces upon their daily lives. The power of the sun was regarded as the great creative force and sustainer of all living things. And the sun god Ra, or Re, was one of their most important deities. Every day the people observed the cycle of the sun's birth, life, and death. Similarly, they witnessed the annual miracle of the river floodwaters' restoring life to the parched land. Osiris, the god of vegetation and king and judge of the Underworld, symbolized the annual rebirth of the land.[31]

Lotus-shaped rays of sunshine emanate from the falcon-headed sun god Ra in a painted wooden panel from ancient Egypt. The people viewed the sun, and its divine representative, as a life-sustaining force.

The fact that Ra, Osiris, and the other gods existed on a plane higher than that of humans seemed a given to the earliest Egyptians. The concept that people's lives were in mysterious ways controlled by such deities was a powerful one. Not surprisingly, the early inhabitants of Egypt wrestled with it and tried to find ways to relate to and serve those divine beings. In this way, a set, standard system of worshiping the gods developed. Over time this made people feel that they occupied their own small, but in its own way special, place in the greater cosmic order.

Visualizing the Gods

A crucial part of that evolving system of worship was the manner in which the early Egyptians visualized the gods. As David Silverman suggests, the way they pictured those higher beings must have developed little by little over time. "At first," he says, "the supreme force would seem awesome and mysterious." Then as people thought more and more about it, they learned to comprehend that force as an entity, or conscious being. At that point, Silverman continues, "it could be recognized, understood, and then reinterpreted in a familiar and recurrent form. In a way, the force could be harnessed. It became humanized. That is, it was put in terms the individual could understand."[32]

Modern scholars believe that this process explains why the earliest Egyptians pictured most of their gods in animal form. In their eyes, those deities were far above and superior to humans and therefore were *not* humans. It thus felt wrong to these early worshipers to envision a god simply as a more powerful form of a human, as the ancient Greeks saw their own gods. Rather, it seemed more proper to the Egyptians to envision the gods as glorious symbols of important nonhuman aspects of nature.

The nonhuman facet of nature those very early Egyptians chose to represent the images of their gods was the physical form of animals. The exact reasons for this choice are unclear, as Rosalie David writes:

> Possibly some animals were worshiped because they assisted humanity, while others, who were feared (such as the jackals who ransacked the cemeteries looking for a meal) were deified in an attempt to appease them. It is evident, however, that animal [forms] were regarded as symbols through which the divine power could manifest itself and that animal worship continued to be extremely important throughout the historic period.[33]

Of the creatures that, in David's words, assisted humanity, the cow proved to be especially important to the Egyptians as a connection to

"The power of the sun was regarded as the great creative force and sustainer of all living things."[31]

—Egyptologist Rosalie David

the divine. In the ancient Nile Valley, cows proved essential to maintaining the local civilization. They were a source of meat, milk, leather, and other products seen as crucial to everyday life. It made sense in Egyptian eyes, therefore, that a cow's physical form might be a symbol—an icon or emblem—for one or more gods. In this way the goddess Hathor came to be depicted as having a cow's head. Similarly, the goddess Bastet had a cat's head; Amun, the head of a ram; Tefnut, a lion's head; Babi, the head of a baboon; Anubis, a jackal's head; and Horus, the head of a falcon.

Religious Beliefs Shaping Life

At first, belief in and worship of these animal-imaged deities was on the local level. Before the emergence of the Egyptian nation, and even before the rise of the Red Land and White Land, the Egyptians dwelled in small individual communities in a sort of tribal existence. So each community or region had certain local gods deemed more important than those of other communities and regions.

This situation changed dramatically when Narmer unified all of Egypt around 3100 BCE. The first pharaoh and his chief advisors brought together the various local gods and the rituals surrounding them into a single, national system. It is unclear exactly how long forging this national religion took, says scholar Leonard H. Lesko. What is certain is that the central government "sought to include almost every god and thereby to satisfy almost every person. It was a product of genius, however, and laid the foundation for one of the longest-lived civilizations in history."[34]

Part of the brilliance of this new religious system was that it did not rob any community or person of long-cherished beliefs. Instead, it artfully combined the gods, beliefs, and rituals from near and far and emphasized their similarities. This approach worked so well because it was inclusive, rather than exclusive. The result was that the Egyptians now had hundreds of deities and a complex, colorful faith steeped in ancient traditions. Moreover, it was based soundly on the notion that the connection between the gods and humans guided the entire workings of the universe, including all aspects of life and death.

The goddess Hathor is depicted with the head of a cow in this modern illustration. Like many of ancient Egypt's deities, Hathor took the physical form of an animal that was essential to daily life.

The aspects of an Egyptian's everyday life that were shaped by religious concepts were nearly all-encompassing. As Lionel Casson wrote, to an average Egyptian

> every detail of his own life, and of the life about him, whether the annual inundation of the Nile that spelled hunger or plenty for the whole nation, or the chance death of his cat, was a specific, calculated act of a god. We of the West can place religion in a compartment of its own. We can say, "Render unto Caesar the things that are Caesar's and to God the things that are God's," but not an Egyptian. His Caesar was the pharaoh, and the pharaoh was a god. Egypt's glorious artistic creations were inspired by religion and religion alone.[35]

Communicating with the Gods

In part because they revered their gods so much, the ancient Egyptians felt compelled to communicate with them at various times. The simplest way this was done, as remains the case in modern faiths, was through prayer. Typically, an Egyptian began his or her prayer with words that followed certain traditional formulas. For instance, he or she might address the god by name and point out one of its well-known attributes—for example: "You are Amun, the Lord of the silent." Then the person praised the god and finally made a formal statement or request. Another common manner of communicating with a god was through an oracle. In the ancient world, it was thought that oracles were people or statues who could convey the words of a god to humans. In ancient Greece, for example, oracles were most often young women. In contrast, the most frequently seen variety of oracle in Egypt was a statue of a deity. Apparently, when someone asked the statue a question, the base on which it stood moved slightly. A forward movement indicated "yes"; a backward movement meant "no." Still another mode of human-divine communication was via dreams. A god supposedly visited a person in a dream and either spoke directly to him or her, or foretold the future by revealing specific visual images. One common dream image was that of a cat, which stood for the following year's harvest. The belief was that the larger the cat, the bigger that harvest would be.

Thus, an Egyptian thought that everything he or she did during a typical day was monitored by one or more gods. If a person did his work well or raised his children properly, the gods knew about it, and that would work in that individual's favor later, after his death. Similarly, if a person committed various bad acts—such as stealing or cheating someone or harming an animal—the gods were aware of those actions, too. Such deeds would of course be held against the person later, when the deities judged whether he or she was worthy of entering the afterlife.

Even in Egyptian politics, government, and the office of the pharaoh, religious beliefs were paramount. The leading government administrators often doubled as high priests in the religious temples. Moreover, the pharaoh himself was initially seen as semidivine, and as such he was expected to fulfill the will of the gods in governing the nation. For example, one of that ruler's most important jobs was to maintain *ma'at* at all times. Ordained by the gods, this was a state of order, harmony, and divine justice thought to exist throughout the universe. The belief was that the gods demanded the preservation of *ma'at* and would punish those who upset it.

Democratizing the Afterlife

No less than their daily lives, the Egyptians' religious beliefs affected their views of death and the afterlife. In fact, as historian Bob Brier aptly states, "no civilization ever devoted so much of its energies and resources to the quest for immortality as did Egypt's."[36] Brier's use of the word *quest* in relation to the afterlife is no accident. Every Egyptian understood that reaching that mysterious post-death realm was not automatic. To the contrary, each person was expected to act in certain positive ways in the *present* life in order to guarantee the survival of his or her soul in the *next* life.

First, it was essential for a person to be as ethical and moral as possible in his or her time on Earth. Certain gods guarded the portal to the underworld. Their job was to judge whether someone was worthy of admission, and they denied entry to people who had led immoral lives. It was also crucial for each person to make preparations for properly preserving and burying his or her body. This need was based on the belief that someone's soul could not be fully maintained unless the body was also suitably preserved in some way.

These beliefs about reaching the afterlife did not preoccupy average Egyptians until around the start of the Middle Kingdom, shortly before 2000 BCE. Evidence suggests that prior to that time the prevailing view was that only the pharaoh could reach the afterlife and achieve immortality. His wives, advisors, and body-servants might be allowed to go with him, only because he required their continued assistance in the next life. All other Egyptians, however, were barred from the afterlife and its benefits. Their souls, if any, simply expired along with their bodies at the moment of death.

It is unclear why this way of thinking faded and entry into the afterlife became democratized to include everyone in society. But there is no doubt that by the early second millennium BCE "every Egyptian in the land, high or humble, came to consider himself eligible for eternal life after death," in Casson's words. "Prayers and rites and way of life" had become the means of reaching the afterlife, "and these were at the disposal of everybody."[37]

Judgment Before Osiris

Still, the "means" of reaching the afterlife was not the same thing as an assurance one would make it there. Each deceased person had to undergo judgment by the divine beings stationed at the underworld's entranceway. These beings included Osiris, lord of that mystifying realm, and a group of his assistants.

Most Egyptians tried to plan ahead for meeting these otherworldly judges by memorizing the so-called negative confession. It consisted of a series of statements, each swearing that a specific sin had not been committed. The belief was that one would need to recite the confession to Osiris and his assistants. It reads in part: "I have not done crimes against people. I have not mistreated cattle. I have not sinned in the Place of Truth," meaning a temple or cemetery, and "I have not insulted a god," or "robbed the poor,"[38] or killed someone, and so forth.

> "Every Egyptian in the land, high or humble, came to consider himself eligible for eternal life after death."[37]
>
> —The late historian Lionel Casson

Complicating matters was that after the person recited the negative confession to Osiris, he or she had to repeat some of its denials to several of that deity's scariest assistants. Among them were characters with names such as "Bone-smasher," "Flame-grasper," and "Fiend from the slaughterhouse." The deceased individual also listed his or her charitable works, if any, to these gruesome beings.

The fate of a person who failed to pass judgment was nothing short of horrendous. Osiris nodded his head and a hideous beast called the "Swallower of the Damned" lurched forward, dragged the screaming individual away, and slowly ate him or her. In contrast, if the per-

As lord of the underworld, Osiris (depicted in an ancient tomb painting) rendered judgment on all who sought to reach the afterlife. How one lived was influenced by the belief that one would eventually undergo this process.

son managed to pass judgment, he or she breathed a sigh of relief and stepped forward into Osiris's kingdom.

Descriptions of that realm of the dead vary in surviving Egyptian literary texts. In the most positive vision, it was a pleasant region located near where the sun rose each day. It was not a paradise, as the Christian and Muslim heaven is usually described. Rather, the Egyptian land of the dead was most often seen as a fairly mundane, Earthlike place where the souls of dead men and women pursued mostly the same professions that they had in life.

Salvation Through Osiris

The deity Osiris was not simply a judge of the dead and overlord of the afterlife. He also had a central role in a concept crucial to ancient Egyptian religion—the salvation of human souls that might lead to their immortal existence following death. Indeed, Osiris made this huge pillar of the faith possible through a harrowing personal sacrifice. A Christlike figure, he suffered an unjust, cruel death, only to be gloriously resurrected later. The tale of this mystical transformation was far and away the most famous and important of ancient Egyptian myths. In that story, not long after the world's creation, the sun god Ra chose Osiris to be Egypt's pharaoh. With the help of his wise and devoted wife, Isis, Osiris became nothing less than a model ruler. But the pharaoh's divine brother, Seth, was envious and resentful of this success and plotted to overthrow Osiris. Not only did Seth slay his royal brother, but he also sliced up the corpse into thousands of pieces and scattered them across Egypt. The murderer was not prepared for loyal and loving Isis's reaction, however. She searched for and found every speck of her slain husband's body and employed powerful magic to resurrect him. Over time, this story inspired the belief that Osiris's death and subsequent rebirth had created a possible path for all Egyptians, royal and nonroyal, to reach the afterlife and enjoy eternal life.

To the ancient Egyptians, therefore, religion was not something to be trotted out once a week at church or to turn to when someone was in trouble and needed a god's help. Beliefs about the gods and the worship of these beings totally permeated an Egyptian's life. They also prepared him or her for their inevitable death and possible salvation to come. As Ian Shaw explains, for an Egyptian there was at all times "an intense sense of the imminence [nearness] of the divine presence." It was "also considered essential to lead one's life on the basis of *ma'at,* the order of the universe, both physical and moral, which came into existence at the creation of the world." To live a decent, ethical life "under the guidance of god brought success in this world and also beyond the grave."[39]

CHAPTER FIVE

How Did Cleopatra Contribute to Ancient Egypt's Final Fall?

Focus Questions

1. Why did Roman rulers seek to dominate Egypt?
2. Why did Cleopatra perceive a need to ally her country with Rome?
3. What might the outcome have been for Egypt if Cleopatra had joined forces with Octavian rather than with Mark Antony?

In 332 BCE, the Macedonian Greek king Alexander III, who later became better known to history as Alexander the Great, arrived in Egypt. He was then on a whirlwind tour of the Middle East, part of his overall attack on the Persian Empire. Indeed, at that point Egypt had been languishing under Persian rule for more than two centuries. So the locals welcomed Alexander as a liberator.

This so-called emancipation proved to be a double-edged sword for the Egyptians, however. Alexander died unexpectedly a mere nine years later and in time his former supporter, the Greek nobleman Ptolemy, took over Egypt, proclaiming himself the pharaoh Ptolemy I. On the positive side, the country was once more an independent nation, and it was still a very rich one. On the negative side, the pharaoh and his leading nobles were Greeks rather than Egyptians. Greek became the official language of the royal court and administration and Greeks came to form a social upper crust, seeing themselves as superior to the natives. Also, as time went on Ptolemaic Egypt became a third-rate country. But despite its weakness, by the mid-first century BCE it was the only major independent nation-state in the Mediterranean sphere that had not been absorbed by the fast-growing Roman realm.

This was the sociopolitical reality into which the last of the Ptolemies, as well as the last Egyptian pharaoh, was born in 69 BCE.

Cleopatra VII was destined on the one hand to at least temporarily raise Egypt back up to a position of power and influence it had not enjoyed in centuries. On the other, however, despite her many talents she was a woman caught in the male-dominated and brutal game of Roman power politics. She also made the mistake of backing the wrong side in a major Roman civil war. That sealed her own fate as well as that of her country.

Power Grabs for Egypt's Throne

Cleopatra was the daughter of Ptolemy XII Auletes, an incompetent, selfish, unpopular ruler whose subjects were often on the brink of rebellion. The general dislike for him was based on his mismanagement of government money and imposition of heavy, unfair taxes on his people. During his reign, Egypt was more or less a Roman client state—that is, a nation economically and militarily dependent on Rome.

Hoping to strengthen his position and repair his image, in 59 BCE Auletes did what several of his royal predecessors had done—turned to rich Roman notables for help. First, he went to the wealthy political rising star Julius Caesar, who bestowed on Auletes the title of "friend and ally" of Rome. The pharaoh hoped that this largely ceremonial title would make him more feared and powerful in Egypt, but it did nothing to aid his poor image as a ruler. What is more, he had been forced to pay Caesar and other Romans large bribes to get that title, which only further depleted Egypt's dwindling treasury.

Growing increasingly anxious, two years later Auletes journeyed to Rome in another attempt to seek foreign aid and support. While he was away, Egypt's government was wracked by a series of power grabs. First, Auletes's daughter Cleopatra Tryphaina (sister of Cleopatra VII) snatched the throne. Some of her father's few remaining supporters quickly killed her. However, another of Cleopatra's sisters, Berenice, then seized power.

With the help of an influential Roman, Auletes managed to get his throne back. But he died soon afterward—in 51 BCE—a despised and unhappy man. His will called for joint rule of Egypt by Cleopatra, now aged eighteen, and her ten-year-old brother, Ptolemy XIII. To her dismay, however, the young woman found herself drawn into a power struggle not of her own making. Her brother and his scheming regent,

A profile of Cleopatra emerges in this carved fragment from Egypt's Ptolemaic period. Egypt's last pharaoh restored her country's power and influence in the world, but that achievement was fleeting.

Pothinus, tried to push her aside so that the boy-king could rule alone. In 49 BCE serious threats to her life forced her to flee the capital—Alexandria—and go into hiding.

Cleopatra, Caesar, and Caesarion

For a while it looked as if young Ptolemy and the underhanded Pothinus had won the fight for Egypt's throne. But then, quite unexpectedly, Cleopatra gained a powerful Roman ally of her own. Julius Caesar, who was in the midst of his own dire fight—a major Roman civil war—suddenly paid a visit to Egypt. He met with Ptolemy and Pothinus and demanded they give him a large sum of money as payment for Auletes's still outstanding debts.

While this was happening, Cleopatra heard about Caesar's arrival and hatched a daring plan to win his support. Their controversial first meeting was summarized by Caesar's ancient biographer, the first-century CE Greek writer Plutarch:

> Taking only one of her friends with her (Apollodorus the Sicilian), [she] embarked in a small boat and landed at the palace when it was already getting dark. Since there seemed to be no other way of getting in, she stretched herself out at full length inside a sleeping bag, and Apollodorus, after tying up the bag, carried it indoors to Caesar. This little trick of Cleopatra's, which showed her provocative impudence, is said to have been the first thing about her which captivated Caesar.[40]

At that moment, Caesar was fifty-two, while Cleopatra was twenty-one. They became lovers, and he supported her in her dispute with her brother. Unwisely, Ptolemy and Pothinus decided to reject Caesar's and Cleopatra's offers to come to some sort of deal and instead tried to fight for the throne. No match for Caesar, they were soon both dead and Cleopatra rose to become pharaoh of Egypt.

"The boy closely resembled Caesar in features as well as in gait [the way he carried himself]."[41]

—Second-century CE Roman historian Suetonius

After enjoying the new queen's hospitality for a few months, Caesar reluctantly returned to prosecuting the civil war. When he left Alexandria early in 47 BCE, she was carrying his child. The next time the lovers met was about a year later, shortly after Caesar had defeated his last rivals and become undisputed master of the Roman realm. He invited Cleopatra and their recently born son to travel to Rome and see the triumphs (military parades) celebrating his recent series of victories. The second-century CE Roman historian Suetonius wrote that Caesar presented Egypt's ruler with "high titles and rich presents." Also, he "allowed her to call the son whom she had borne him by his own name." This name was Caesarion, although his official Egyptian title was Ptolemy XV. "The boy closely resembled Caesar," Suetonius said, "in features as well as in gait [the way he carried himself]."[41]

Caesar never got a chance to get to know his son. On March 15, 44 BCE, while Cleopatra and the child were still in Rome, a group of Roman senators assassinated him. (They were upset that he had recently proclaimed himself dictator for life, which they rightly viewed as a threat to their own power.) On hearing the awful news of her lover's death, Cleopatra prudently gathered her son and sailed back to Egypt.

Angered by Julius Caesar's decision to proclaim himself dictator for life, a group of Roman senators kill their powerful leader. His assassination presented new dangers for Cleopatra, who had been Caesar's lover and had borne him a son.

Cleopatra's Decree Regarding Taxes

That Cleopatra was a fair and effective ruler is suggested by the contents of a few surviving documents from her reign. One is a decree regarding the subject of taxes, issued in 41 BCE. In it, she said that no one should demand anything of the nation's farmers beyond the existing taxes they paid. Further, she stated that she was "extremely indignant" about any overtaxing of the people and considered it "well to issue a general and universal ordinance," or regulation, "regarding the whole matter." Also, "I have decreed that all those from the cities, who carry on agricultural work in the country, shall not be subjected, as others are, to demands for *stephanoi* and *epigraphai*." These were gifts and special taxes her predecessors had forced farmers and others to give the government from time to time. The queen went on:

> Nor shall any new tax be required of them. But when they have once paid the essential dues, in kind [in the form of goods and services] or in cash, for cornfields and for vineyards, [they] shall not be molested for anything further, on any pretext whatever. Let it be done accordingly, and this decree put up in public, according to Law.

Quoted in Jack Lindsay, *Cleopatra*. London: Folio Society, 2004, pp. 127–28.

Cleopatra, Antony, and Octavian

Although now far away from Rome, the Egyptian queen had spies who kept her informed about the turbulent events that occurred in the wake of Caesar's demise. At first, Caesar's military assistant, Mark Antony; Caesar's eighteen-year-old adopted son, Octavian; and the popular general Marcus Lepidus formed a pact known as the Second Triumvirate. They slew many of their political opponents, including the leaders of the conspiracy against Caesar. Then the three triumvirs divided up the Roman-controlled Mediterranean world among themselves. Antony took charge of the "East," consisting of Rome's provinces in Greece and the Middle East, then the richest and most populous sector of the Roman realm. Octavian, who would eventually become Antony's chief rival, received Rome's western portions, including Spain, Gaul (France), Italy, and the capital city itself. Lepidus got parts of North Africa.

Because the still independent Egypt bordered the lands that Antony now controlled, it was probably inevitable that he and Cleopatra would get to know each other in one way or another. Indeed, in the summer of 41 BCE he found himself

"She came sailing up the river Cydnus in a barge with a stern of gold, its purple sails billowing in the wind."[42]

—First-century CE Greek writer Plutarch

badly in need of her ample supplies of money and grain. So he beckoned her to meet him in Tarsus, in southern Anatolia (now Turkey). Her colorful approach to his headquarters there has become the stuff of legend. According to Plutarch,

> She came sailing up the river Cydnus in a barge with a stern of gold, its purple sails billowing in the wind, while her rowers caressed the water with oars of silver which dipped in time to the music of the flute, accompanied by pipes and lutes. Cleopatra herself reclined beneath a canopy of gold cloth, dressed as Venus [goddess of love]. On either side [of her] stood boys costumed as Cupids, who cooled her with fans. Instead of a crew, her barge was lined with the most beautiful of her waiting-women attired as [minor goddesses], some at the rudders, other at the [sails], and all the while an indescribably rich perfume [drifted] from the vessel to the river-banks. Great multitudes [of local people] accompanied this royal progress, some of them following the queen on both sides of the river from its very mouth, while others hurried down from the city of Tarsus to gaze at the sight.[42]

King and Queen of the World?

The hard-drinking, rough-mannered, and already married Antony found Cleopatra captivating, and after their meeting in Tarsus the two almost immediately became lovers and allies. At first, however, they did not spend much time together. He was an ambitious soldier who wanted to conquer new lands for Rome, and she was a sincere queen who made ruling her country her top priority.

In fact, convincing evidence shows that Cleopatra was a skilled, efficient ruler who managed the economy well and treated her subjects fairly. Unlike the reigns of her immediate Ptolemaic ancestors, hers was productive, and her personality, style of rule, and deeds fomented no threats of rebellion. The hardworking queen increased the nation's already impressive output of grain and other foodstuffs. She also became fluent in Demotic Egyptian, the local language, a feat none of the earlier Ptolemies had bothered to accomplish. Moreover, in an attempt to connect with ordinary Egyptians, she used that tongue along with Greek in the royal court.

In addition Cleopatra impressed her people with her earnest observances of Egyptian religious rites. In these endeavors she depicted herself as the earthly envoy of the widely loved mother and fertility goddess Isis. Besides aiding the growth of wheat and barley, that deity was thought to forgive worshipers' sins and help purify their souls. Cleopatra even went so far as to appear in the guise of Isis, as Egyptian artists had long portrayed her, during public religious ceremonies. Plutarch described how she "wore the robe which is sacred to Isis, and she was addressed as the New Isis."[43]

Cleopatra was dressed as Isis when she and her lover-ally, Antony, staged a massive public display in Alexandria. "They assembled a great multitude in the athletic arena there," Plutarch reported, "and had two thrones of gold, one for himself and one for Cleopatra, placed on a dais [platform] of silver."[44] This magnificent ceremony seemed to proclaim far and wide that Antony and Cleopatra fancied themselves the king and queen of the known world.

Cleopatra's Calculated Risk

Whether or not the lovers actually intended to represent themselves that way, most observers, both inside and outside of Egypt, assumed they did. Particularly offended was Octavian, who felt that Antony had disgraced himself by allowing a "corrupt" foreign woman to rob him of his common sense and Roman morals and decency.

Cleopatra stands with her troops at the Battle of Actium. The battle ended in a crushing defeat for Cleopatra and Mark Antony and marked the end of Egypt's independence in the ancient world.

Cleopatra was well aware that this negative image of her had become part of Octavian's official stream of propaganda. He had increasingly come to see Antony as a poor administrator and unreliable ally, and thereby a threat to both himself and Rome. At the same time, Egypt was still a very rich country. In Octavian's view, there seemed good reason to believe that Cleopatra might use that wealth to back

A Pitiable Sight

After Octavian and his troops landed near Alexandria, the city fell temporarily into chaos. In the midst of this confusion, someone incorrectly told Antony that Cleopatra was dead. Hearing this, he tried to kill himself by plunging his sword into his abdomen. But death did not come immediately. Meanwhile, the queen found out about his condition and sent some servants to bring him to her in her tomb, which was still under construction. She was afraid that if she unlocked the doors the Romans might gain entry. So she ordered that Antony's body be raised via ropes to an open window where she waited. Basing his account on the description of an earlier writer, Plutarch described the scene, saying,

> There was never a more pitiable sight than the spectacle of Antony, covered with blood, struggling in his death agonies and stretching out his hands toward Cleopatra as he swung helplessly in the air. The task was almost beyond a woman's strength, and it was only with great difficulty that Cleopatra, clinging with both hands to the rope and with the muscles of her face distorted by the strain, was able to haul him up, while those on the ground encouraged her and shared her agony. When she had got him up and laid him upon a bed, she tore her dress and spread it over him, beat and lacerated her breasts, and smeared her face with the blood from his wounds.

Antony soon died in her arms, and a few days later she took her own life.

Plutarch, *Life of Antony*, in *Makers of Rome: Nine Lives by Plutarch*, trans. Ian Scott-Kilvert. New York: Penguin, 1965, pp. 341–42.

a power grab of western Rome by Antony. This view was essentially correct. Cleopatra did decide to back Antony against his rival. It was a very calculated risk on her part because if she chose the wrong side, both she and her country would surely end up paying dearly.

Whatever the chief players in this power game may have been thinking, the Second Triumvirate steadily fell apart, and a civil war between Octavian in the West and Antony and Cleopatra in the East erupted in 32 BCE. (By this time, Octavian had eliminated the third member of the triumvirate, Marcus Lepidus, by placing him under house arrest.) The Egyptian queen and her Roman lover-ally were at first quite confident of victory. After all, it was common knowledge that they had considerably more money, soldiers, warships, and food supplies than Octavian.

But Octavian had some key advantages of his own. First, he was assisted by a skilled, insightful, and experienced military commander—Marcus Agrippa. Also, Octavian, who was more calculating than Antony, seized the initiative. He wisely moved his forces into the eastern Mediterranean before Cleopatra and Antony had time to properly organize their own army and navy. Agrippa then deftly trapped the lovers' navy near Actium, in western Greece.

Cleopatra and Antony now had no other choice but to engage in a major sea battle in order to break free. Fought on September 2, 31 BCE, that single clash determined the outcome of the entire war. The Egyptian queen and her Roman partner endured a crushing defeat, although they, along with a handful of followers, were able to escape and make it back to Egypt.

Rome's Heavy Hand

Cleopatra and Antony knew full well that they were in serious trouble. Their one chance of turning things around was to use Egypt's national treasury to build a new fleet, seek aid from nearby eastern lands, and launch a new offensive. But this proved a vain hope. Most of Antony's troops deserted him, and all of Cleopatra's neighbors saw the lovers' crusade against Rome as a lost cause and abandoned them.

Now in desperate straits, Cleopatra thought she might save her country by making a deal of some kind with Octavian. To that end, she offered him huge bribes to keep him from advancing on Egypt. But such attempts to halt the inevitable failed. Octavian landed his army not far from Alexandria in July 30 BCE, and not long afterward, first Antony and then Cleopatra took their own lives.

At her death, Cleopatra was only thirty-nine years old. During her tenure as Egypt's pharaoh she had shown herself to be a smart, skilled, ambitious, and gutsy ruler. Ultimately, her fatal mistake was backing the wrong Roman. This blunder proved disastrous for Egypt as well,

"Through her own unaided genius, she captivated the two greatest Romans of her time."[45]

—Second-century CE Greek historian Dio Cassius

for Octavian annexed that land as a Roman province, and no new pharaoh took Cleopatra's place. Ancient Egypt's long tradition of independence, interrupted only briefly in the past, was now over for good.

Rome's spectacular rise to world dominance had made this sad destiny for Egypt almost unavoidable. Rome's heavy hand in bringing about that once proud nation's demise is well illustrated in the second-century CE Greek historian Dio Cassius's now famous remark about the last Egyptian pharaoh. "Through her own unaided genius," he wrote, "she captivated the two greatest Romans of her time; and because of the third, she destroyed herself."[45]

Introduction: The Battle of the Animals

1. Herodotus, *Histories,* trans. Aubrey de Sélincourt. New York: Penguin, 2003, p. 155.
2. Polyaenus, *Strategems of War,* trans. Richard Shepherd, adapt. Andrew Smith. http://attalus.org/translate/polyaenus7.html.
3. Polyaenus, *Strategems of War.*
4. Herodotus, *Histories,* p. 207.

Chapter One: A Brief History of Ancient Egypt

5. David P. Silverman, "The Lord of the Two Lands," in David P. Silverman, ed., *Ancient Egypt.* New York: Oxford University Press, 1997, p. 108.
6. H.W.F. Saggs, *Civilization Before Greece and Rome.* New Haven, CT: Yale University Press, 1991, p. 25.
7. Dieter Arnold, *Building in Egypt: Pharaonic Stone Masonry.* Oxford: Oxford University Press, 1991, p. 4.
8. Quoted in John L. Foster, trans., *Ancient Egyptian Literature.* Austin: University of Texas Press, 2001, pp. 33–34.
9. Quoted in W.K. Simpson, ed., *The Literature of Ancient Egypt: An Anthology of Stories, Instructions, and Poetry.* New Haven, CT: Yale University Press, 2003, pp. 61–62.
10. Chester G. Starr, *A History of the Ancient World.* New York: Oxford University Press, 1991, p. 89.
11. Zahi A. Hawass, *The Mysteries of Abu Simbel: Ramesses II and the Temples of the Rising Sun.* Cairo, Egypt: American University in Cairo Press, 2001, pp. 44, 48.
12. Toby Wilkinson, *The Rise and Fall of Ancient Egypt.* New York: Random House, 2010, pp. 485–86.

Chapter Two: How Did the Nile River Make Egyptian Civilization Possible?

13. Ian Shaw and Paul Nicholson, *The Dictionary of Ancient Egypt.* New York: Harry N. Abrams, 2003, p. 202.

14. Charles Gates, *Ancient Cities: The Archaeology of Urban Life in the Ancient Near East and Egypt, Greece, and Rome*. London: Routledge, 2007, p. 79.
15. Herodotus, *Histories*, p. 131.
16. Quoted in Miriam Lichtheim, ed., *Ancient Egyptian Literature: A Book of Readings*, vol. 1. Berkeley: University of California Press, 1975, p. 208.
17. Exodus 2:5.
18. Eugen Strouhal, *Life of the Ancient Egyptians*. Norman: University of Oklahoma Press, 1992, p. 75.
19. Quoted in Strouhal, *Life of the Ancient Egyptians*, p. 123.
20. Quoted in Strouhal, *Life of the Ancient Egyptians*, p. 123.
21. Seneca, *Natural Questions*, excerpted in C.D.N. Costa, trans. and ed., *Seneca: Dialogues and Letters*. New York: Penguin, 1997, p. 110.
22. Seneca, *Natural Questions*, p. 110.
23. Lionel Casson, *Daily Life in Ancient Egypt*. New York: American Heritage, 1994, p. 35.

Chapter Three: How Did an Agrarian Society Build Some of the World's Most Enduring Structures?
24. Zahi Hawass, "The Discovery of the Tombs of the Pyramid Builders at Giza," Guardian's Egypt. www.guardians.net/hawass/build tomb.htm.
25. Zahi Hawass, "Tombs of the Pyramid Builders," *Archaeology*, January/February 1997, pp. 39–43.
26. Kate Spence, "The Great Sphinx at Giza," in *The Seventy Wonders of the Ancient World*, ed. Chris Scarre. London: Thames and Hudson, 1999, p. 25.
27. Spence, "The Great Sphinx at Giza," p. 25.
28. Robert M. Schoch, *Pyramid Quest: Secrets of the Great Pyramid and the Dawn of Civilization*. New York: Penguin, 2005, p. 97.
29. Herodotus, *Histories*, p. 179.

Chapter Four: How Did Religious Beliefs Shape Egyptian Views of Life and Death?
30. Herodotus, *Histories*, p. 143.

31. Rosalie David, *Handbook to Life in Ancient Egypt.* New York: Facts On File, 2007, p. 59.

32. David P. Silverman, "Divinity and Deities in Ancient Egypt," in Byron E. Shafer, ed., *Religion in Ancient Egypt.* Ithaca, NY: Cornell University Press, 1991, pp. 17–18.

33. David, *Handbook to Life in Ancient Egypt,* p. 101.

34. Leonard H. Lesko, "Ancient Egyptian Cosmogonies and Cosmology," in Byron E. Shafer, ed., *Religion in Ancient Egypt.* Ithaca, NY: Cornell University Press, 1991, pp. 90–91.

35. Casson, *Daily Life in Ancient Egypt,* pp. 79–80.

36. Bob Brier, "Egyptomania: What Accounts for Our Intoxication with Things Egyptian?," *Archaeology,* January/February 2004, p. 18.

37. Casson, *Daily Life in Ancient Egypt,* pp. 103–104.

38. Quoted in Miriam Lichtheim, ed., *Ancient Egyptian Literature: A Book of Readings,* vol. 2. Berkeley: University of California Press, 2006, pp. 124–26.

39. Ian Shaw, *The Oxford History of Ancient Egypt.* New York: Oxford University Press, 2002, pp. 391–92.

Chapter Five: How Did Cleopatra Contribute to Ancient Egypt's Final Fall?

40. Plutarch, *Life of Caesar,* in *Fall of the Roman Republic: Six Lives by Plutarch,* trans. Rex Warner. New York: Penguin, 1972, p. 290.

41. Suetonius, *Julius Caesar,* in *Lives of the Twelve Caesars.* Published as *The Twelve Caesars,* trans. Robert Graves, rev. Michael Grant. New York: Penguin, 1979, p. 36.

42. Plutarch, *Life of Antony,* in *Makers of Rome: Nine Lives by Plutarch,* trans. Ian Scott-Kilvert. New York: Penguin, 1965, p. 293.

43. Plutarch, *Life of Antony,* p. 322.

44. Plutarch, *Life of Antony,* p. 322.

45. Dio Cassius, *Roman History,* in *The Roman History: The Reign of Augustus,* trans. Ian Scott-Kilvert. New York: Penguin, 1987, p. 76.

Books

L.J. Amstutz and Lisa Amstutz, *Ancient Egypt*. Edina, MN: Essential Library, 2015.

Charlotte Booth, *Lost Voices of the Nile: Everyday Life in Ancient Egypt*. Stroud, UK: Amberley, 2017.

Bernard Green, *Building the Khufu Pyramids*. Seattle: Amazon Digital, 2016.

Roy Jackson, *Egypt: Egyptian Mythology and the Secrets of the Gods*. Seattle: Amazon Digital, 2016.

Don Nardo, *Life in Ancient Egypt*. San Diego, CA: ReferencePoint, 2015.

Vicky A. Shecter, *Cleopatra Rules! The Amazing Life of the Original Teen Queen*. Honesdale, PA: Boyds Mills, 2013.

Websites

The Ancient Egypt Site (www.ancient-egypt.org). Created and maintained by Jacques Kinnaer, a noted Belgian Egyptologist, this large, outstanding collection of web pages and links relates to ancient Egypt, including history, language, monuments, religion, and much more.

BBC History, "Egyptians" (www.bbc.co.uk/history/ancient/egyptians). The BBC presents a high-quality website, providing links to several major aspects of ancient Egyptian history, life, and arts.

Discovering Ancient Egypt (http://discoveringegypt.com). Mark Millmore, an expert on ancient Egyptian art, manages and writes the text for this excellent site, which has links to topics such as "Egyptian Gods," "Hieroglyphs," and "Temples in 3D."

History.com, "Ancient Egypt" (www.history.com/topics/ancient -history/ancient-egypt). This colorful website features links to articles and videos pertaining to various aspects of ancient Egyptian history and culture.

Live Science, "Ancient Egypt: A Brief History" (www.livescience .com/55578-egyptian-civilization.html). New York–based Live Science, a website created by professional science reporters, offers this valuable look at ancient Egypt. In addition to facts about history and culture, the site has links to fascinating articles with titles such as "Hidden King Tut Chamber," "Pyramid Interior Revealed," and "Oldest Depiction of Ancient Egyptian Demons."

PBS *NOVA*: "The Afterlife in Ancient Egypt" (www.pbs.org/wgbh /nova/ancient/afterlife-ancient-egypt.html). This worthwhile web page explores the Egyptians' unique beliefs about the afterlife and includes links to articles about diverse aspects of mummification.